# PERSONS

# PERSONS

*A Study in Philosophical Psychology*

RAZIEL ABELSON

*Professor of Philosophy*
*New York University*

*First published 1977 by*
THE MACMILLAN PRESS LTD

*London and Basingstoke*
*Associated companies in New York*
*Dublin Melbourne Johannesburg and Madras*

ISBN 0 333 21415 3

*Printed in Great Britain by*
WESTERN PRINTING SERVICES LTD
*Bristol*

W 1336 /8.95 11.77

To Gabriel

'Everybody has to be somebody to somebody, in order to be anybody.'
(Forbes, in *Reader's Digest*)

# Contents

*Acknowledgements*                                                          ix

*Introduction*                                                              xi

1   Conceptual Dualism                                                      1
    Psychological Language                                                 2
    Psychological Explanation                                              7

2   Authority and Freedom to Avow                                         13
    Types of Self-Descriptions and the Role of Avowals                    14
    Avowals Proper                                                        17
    Avowals and Psychological Generalisations                            21
    Incorrigibility                                                       24

3   Cause and Reason                                                      28
    The Conceptual Revolution                                            29
    Causes and Reasons                                                   30
    Doing, Causing and Causing-to-do                                     36

4   Motivation                                                           48
    Reasons and Reason Terminators                                       48
    Reason Terminators and Explanation                                   51
    Reasons, Desires and Feelings                                        53
    Emotion                                                              57

5   The Incoherence of Determinism                                       62
    The Irrelevance Defence                                              62
    The Dualistic Interaction Defence                                    64
    The Identity Defence                                                 67
    Objections and Replies                                               69

6   Person and Self                                                       74
    P-Predicates                                                         76
    Personal Identity and Self                                           85

7   Self-Deception and *Akrasia*                                          94
    The Paradoxes of Self-Deception                                      94
    Proposed Solutions                                                   96
    A Synthesis                                                          98
    A New Start                                                         102
    Weakness of Will                                                    106

## Contents

8   Self and Community     110
      Self-Interest and Morality     111
      Conclusions     118

*Notes*     119

*Selected Bibliography*     127

*Index of Names*     131

*Index of Subjects*     134

# Acknowledgements

I am grateful to the American Council of Learned Societies and to the Arts and Science Research Fund of New York University for grants enabling me to prepare this volume.

I wish to thank the *Journal of Philosophy*, the *American Philosophical Quarterly*, *Mind* and *Philosophical Studies* (Reidel) for their kind permission to reprint portions of articles of mine that have appeared in those journals. Thanks are also due to Basil Blackwell and Mott Ltd for permission to use extracts from *Philosophical Investigations* by Ludwig Wittgenstein.

I am indebted to my friends, Professor Chauncey Downes, of New York University, and Professor Michael Lockwood, of All Souls College, Oxford, for their patient reading of earlier drafts and for their helpful comments.

I would like also to express my appreciation for the valuable criticisms I received of sections of this work when read to the faculty and students of the following colleges and universities: New York University, Cornell University, SUNY Binghamton, University of Pittsburgh, University of California at Berkeley, University of California at Santa Barbara, University of Southern California, Long Island University, Hamilton College, Rutgers University, William Paterson College and Suffolk County Community College.

R.A.

# Introduction

For some years I had been working on particular problems in philosophy of mind surrounding the concept of reason-giving, problems into which I was led by earlier studies in ethical reasoning. In various papers I had explored the concepts of emotion, feeling and wanting, the differences between rational explanation and scientific explanation, the relations between knowledge, belief and faith, and the paradoxes of mind-body identity theories. At some point, all these pieces seemed to fall together into a general picture, which I have here baptised 'Conceptual Dualism', in which the human agent appears as a creative force intervening in an otherwise deterministic world, somewhat as God was once thought to do (arbitrarily, for Duns Scotus, rationally for Aquinas and Leibniz). The combined attacks on dualism and mechanism by ordinary language philosophers (Wittgenstein, Ryle, Austin), which punctured the modern mythology of scientific determinism, and their demonstrations of the extraordinarily subtle logic of ordinary language (compared to which mathematical logic appears a crude approximation, somewhat like a computer grinding out a soap opera scenario as compared to *The Brothers Karamazov*) convinced me that a transformation of our vision of man and his place in nature has been taking place and is now ready to be formally inaugurated as the New Order.

The guiding principle of this conceptual revolution has been the recognition of the normative character of the language in which we describe human conduct. Normative judgments are, for good reason, eschewed by natural science as irrelevant to its theories, laws, and predictions. When a natural scientist allows himself the luxury of value judgments he does so during coffee breaks, or after hours when reading *The Times* or complaining to his (or her) spouse. Yet, in anything intelligible we say about human conduct, we express or at least presuppose judgments of good and bad, right and wrong, successful and unsuccessful, judgments that, when not mere prejudices, are grounded on reasons which in turn may be evaluated as good or bad.

Until this revolution in philosophy got under way in the second quarter of this century, almost all philosophers (with the exceptions of Hume and Kant) assumed that ethics is an applied science, based on biology, history and psychology. The conceptual revolution of which (and for which) I speak consists in a reversal of this classical perspective (perhaps this is the real Kantian 'Copernican revolution', although some sceptics would call it the Ptolemaic counter-revolution) a recognition that we have been envisioning the human world upside down, for the concepts of psychology and social science, if they are to apply to human reality, must be defined in terms of normative concepts such as good and bad, skilful and clumsy, right and wrong. The language of action is quite distinct from that of scientific observation and explanation. But the two are not separate and equal; the former underlies, justifies and sets limits to the latter. Ethics is not the queen of the sciences, but their *raison d'être*. This was the profound insight of American pragmatism (James, Peirce and Dewey), revived and strengthened by the commonsense contextualism of British ordinary language analysis and, in a different idiom, Sartrian existentialism.

In the study that follows, I have tried to fit together the pieces of the conceptual puzzle into as clear a picture as I can construct, whereby the irruptions of human creativity into the (macroscopic) deterministic order of nature are explainable in terms quite different from those scientific creations of man himself (laws and theories) by which natural phenomena are described, predicted and explained. I begin by exploring the differences between psychological explanation and natural scientific explanation in terms of intentionality, non-observational self-ascription and normative judgment. In Chapter 2, I try to show how psychological explanation rests ultimately on avowals, which bring into existence the basic data of our knowledge of ourselves, and how this socially bestowed authority of avowal sets limits to the causal determinism of natural science, making it logically impossible to capture voluntary human action in the net of causal explanation.

In Chapter 3 I explore the differences between reasons and causes, in terms of the types and purposes of the explanations they provide. I argue that the 'language game' of reason-giving involves criticism and justification, blaming and excusing, attributions of merit and demerit that have no place in the 'language game' of causal explanation. The concept of voluntary human action is the central concept of this reason-giving language game, and action discourse should not therefore be confused with causal discourse. The central argument for this 'conceptual dualist' view of action discourse was first formulated by A. I. Melden. I consider various objections to Melden's 'logical connection' argument by science-oriented philosophers, and reformulations of the argument by Richard Taylor, and then I develop a refinement of the argument in terms of the notion of 'contextual entailment' which, I believe, escapes the difficulties pointed out by Davidson, Gean, and other defenders of universal causality. The crucial step in my argument is a distinction, heretofore unnoticed, between the concepts of causing-to-do and plain causing.

In Chapter 4 I apply the preceding analysis to the explanation of the logical role in action-explanations of 'reason-terminating locutions' such as 'because I want to', and then of motivational concepts such as emotion, feeling, desire and motive. All of these modes of description and explanation, I argue, involve rational evaluation, but in different ways. Reason-terminating locutions indicate that rational justification is not required, or that the lack of such justification is excusable (e.g. 'irresistible impulse'). Feelings are states of neural excitation identified by the agent in terms of his evaluation of the situation (e.g. a twinge of fear, excitement, envy, hope, etc.). Desires are tendencies to actions for specific reasons, usually attended by appropriate feelings. Emotions are extraordinarily complex melanges of action-dispositions, evaluations of provocative circumstances and systems of value-priorities. Ascriptions of emotions thus imply considerable information about an agent's character and values. Needless to say such ascriptions are usually unreliable guesses, unless supported by intimate knowledge of the agent.

The crucial metaphysical issue raised by conceptual dualism is then directly faced in Chapter 5: Are these two modes of discourse – psychological discourse about actions and their reasons, on the one side, and natural-scientific discourse about events and their causes on the other side – co-equal and equivalent, as 'dual aspect' and 'identity' theories of metaphysics have maintained, or does the irrelevance of causality to human action entail indeterminism, i.e. gaps in the causal chains of nature wherever voluntary human action intervenes? Most of the philosophers whose insights have led to the philosophy of conceptual dualism (Ryle, Melden, C. Taylor, Kenny, Anscombe, R. Taylor, Macintyre, Winch, with the conspicuous exception of R. Peters) have shied away from the indeterministic precipice toward which they have led us. I argue against such excessive timidity, and in favour of the leap into metaphysical indeterminism. I argue first that a decision between determinism and indeterminism cannot be avoided by appealing, as Melden and R. Taylor do, to the impossibility of translating action language into physical event language, since every human action is extensionally identical to some physical event. Next, I argue that any interactionist appeal to 'internal' mental causes of action, in an effort to extend determinism to human action without sacrificing the distinctions between action discourse and event discourse, results in self-contradiction. Finally, I consider the most popular view of the relation between psychology and physics, namely, mind-body identity theory, and I offer a mathematical proof of the absurdity of any such theory. It follows that, as Kant suggested, man, insofar as he acts rationally, is not a phenomenon governed by causal laws, but a noumenon guided by rules of his own creation.

But if man is not a natural phenomenon, not just an intelligent animal, then what sort of entity is he? What is this human 'noumenon'? Chapter 6 develops the conception of man as a person, endowed with the capacity to see himself and his fellowmen as free and responsible agents, as authors of their own actions, avowals, goals and reasons. Following Strawson's analysis of the concept of a person as indefinable in terms of necessary and sufficient properties, and defending this insight against A. J. Ayer's criticisms, I suggest that the concept of a person is a status-concept, analogous to more specific status concepts such as governor, judge, doctor, spouse and friend, in fact, constituting the genus of which these social roles are species. I then argue for the importance of distinguishing the concept of 'self' from that of 'person', and suggest that the concept of self has two uses, one of which is the trivial grammatical role of self-reference, while the more philosophically interesting use is that explained by Sartre and Freud as a projection of one's future goals.

The analysis of the meaning of 'self' is applied, in Chapter 7, to the resolution of the paradoxes of self-deception. Four attempts to resolve these paradoxes are discussed and shown to be inadequate, namely Freud's multiple self model, Sartre's dialectical model, the translational theories of several analytical philosophers (Demos, Siegler, Gustafson and Penelhum – adequately criticised by H. Fingarette), and finally, Fingarette's self-amputation model. I then offer a synthesis of the partial insights of these four approaches, in terms of a distinction between first and second order acts of self-deception which, in turn, centres on the Melden–Danto distinction, introduced in Chapter 3, between basic and complex actions. Although the paradoxes of self-deception appear, on this new account, to be resolvable, it turns out that one piece of the puzzle still eludes us. The last piece is provided, but only in outline, since we find that it can only be fleshed out by the avowals of the agent who possesses adequate self-knowledge. In the final chapter, the philosophical sense of 'self' explored in Chapters 6 and 7 is applied to the definition of 'self-knowledge' and 'self-interest', concepts that are shown to presuppose a community of moral agents whose avowals of their self-interests constitute *prima facie* reasons for action. It follows that morality and self-interest converge, and this fact provides the answer to the question 'Why should we be moral?' Thus the concept of a person entails that of a moral community of autonomous agents, each of whom recognises the rights and interests of all others.

The path I have followed in this work was lighted by Ludwig Wittgenstein's *Philosophical Investigations*, although the first road-map was drawn by Ryle's *Concept of Mind*. I have acknowledged my debt to Ryle in references throughout this book, but since Wittgenstein refrained from theoretical generalisations, I cannot claim his authority for the theory of persons offered here. I have thought it appropriate, therefore, to indicate my debt to Wittgenstein by beginning each chapter with a remark from his writings and conversations that has suggested to me the view I have taken in the chapter.

# 1  Conceptual Dualism

'Why can't a dog simulate pain? Is he too honest?' – Wittgenstein, *Philosophical Investigations*

'The confusion and barrenness of psychology is not to be explained by calling it a "going science"; its state is not comparable with that of physics, for instance, in its beginning . . . For in psychology there are experiments, methods and *conceptual confusion*' – Ibid., pt II

Recent studies in the conceptual foundations of psychology, beginning with Gilbert Ryle's *The Concept of Mind* and Ludwig Wittgenstein's *Philosophical Investigations*, have disclosed some interesting differences between the language of natural science and the language in which we describe human experiences and actions – differences that were vaguely sensed by Kant when he contrasted the realm of nature with the realm of freedom. The dominant tendency in experimental psychology is to disregard these differences and to assimilate psychological concepts to the language of natural science by means of operational definitions. In so doing, psychologists like Tolman, Hull, Skinner and Hebb reduce psychology to biology. (In fact, Hebb explicitly defines psychology as 'a branch of biology'.[1]) Clinical, social and analytical psychologists, on the other hand, continue to do non-biological psychology, but with uneasy consciences. When they claim for their work the same kind of scientific warrant that is claimed by experimental psychologists, they tend to repudiate the very features of human psychology that distinguish it as psychological. To sum up the matter roughly and provisionally: to the degree to which a psychologist tries to be scientific in a way analogous to physicists and biologists, to that degree his procedure is self-defeating, for it will not produce positive *psychological* knowledge. Experimental psychologists are very scientific in this sense, and that is probably why they have added little to our knowledge of *human* motivation, although they have found out a great deal about physiology and animal behaviour. Clinical, social and analytical psychologists often discover very interesting facts about human motivation, but only, I believe, when they are not trying to construct or verify a scientific theory. In what follows, I shall try to account for this apparent paradox, and then to draw some consequences for the methodology of psychological inquiry.

## PSYCHOLOGICAL LANGUAGE

Why do words like 'believe', 'motive', 'anger' and 'feeling' belong on a list of psychological terms, while 'round', 'mutation', 'magnetic' and 'electronic' do not? There may be many reasons, but I would like to consider three that have been emphasised in recent philosophical discussions. These reasons are: (1) that psychological terms are those which a person can apply to himself without observation, (2) that their correct application essentially involves normative judgment, and (3) that they are intentional concepts.

### Non-observational self-ascription

G. E. M. Anscombe, P. F. Strawson and Sidney Shoemaker[2] have suggested that the distinguishing feature of psychological language is that it can be applied by a speaker to himself without prior observation of what he, the speaker, is doing, while it can be applied to others only by observing their behaviour. I can say truly that Smith is suffering pain only after watching Smith's facial expressions and actions, or hearing him groan or say that he is in pain, but I can say truly that *I* am suffering pain without watching myself in a mirror, or listening to my own voice. In contrast, I cannot know that I am moving through space with a certain velocity, or that I weigh 150 pounds, or that my body is composed of cells, without observing my body and its relation to other objects. We may sum up the differences by saying that in psychology, self-knowledge has privileged authority over knowledge of others, while in natural science, all knowledge rests equally on controlled observation. Nineteenth-century introspectionist psychologists like Wundt and Titchener correctly noted this fact, but they drew two unfortunate conclusions: (1) that self-knowledge is indubitable, a conclusion which is clearly false, and (2) that self-knowledge involves introspection or inward observation of a ghostly realm of mental events. This obscure explanation of the clear fact that each person has privileged knowledge of himself was rightly abandoned by behavioural psychologists who unfortunately threw out the baby with the bath water. In rejecting the obscure doctrine of introspection, they also closed their eyes to the very important fact that psychological beings do have non-observational self-knowledge, and they held that psychology is exclusively knowledge of the observational behaviour of others, relegating self-knowledge to the humiliating status of 'verbal behaviour' (a term made current by B. F. Skinner). The well-known joke about the psychologist who meets a colleague and asks politely, 'How am I?', is a *reductio ad absurdum* of the notion that self-descriptions are conditioned responses symptomatic of the state of the speaker, but no more worthy of belief than the barking of a dog.

One need only note the dependence of psychological inquiry on questionnaires, interviews and other types of self-reports to see that the reliability of most of our self-descriptions is an essential condition for the very existence of a science of psychology. If subjects could not tell us what they see, there would be no science of perception; if they could not tell us how they feel and what they want, there would be no knowledge of motivation; if they could not tell us what they believe and what they dream, there would be no psychiatry. Behaviourists might reply to this argument by pointing out that they have discovered a good deal of information about animal psychology even though animals cannot talk about themselves. But it seems doubtful that we could know anything about the psychological states of animals if it were not for their resemblances to human beings who do talk about themselves. Animal behaviour sufficiently resembles certain stereotyped patterns of human behaviour so that we feel justified in describing animals in the same terms by which we describe ourselves – as angry, depressed, fearful, hungry, intelligent, and the like. But the obvious limitations on this kind of analogical reasoning from our own states to those of animals have led behavioural psychologists to take refuge in technical jargon which, for some inexplicable reason, they still call 'psychology'. For if the technical vocabulary of 'reinforcement', 'stimulus-response', 'tension reduction', etc. is detached from the language of non-observational self-description that gives it its psychological content, it becomes hard to see what there is for psychology to explain that physiology and physics cannot take care of without its help.

*Normative judgment*

A second peculiarity of psychological language that distinguishes it from the language of natural science was emphasised by Richard Peters in his monograph, *The Concept of Motivation*, and Peter Winch, in *The Idea of a Social Science*,[3] although it was first suggested by Gilbert Ryle in *The Concept of Mind*.[4] Psychological concepts apply only to creatures that exhibit certain skills. 'Perceives', 'knows', 'responds', 'avoids' are descriptions that imply some kind of ability even in failure. A rat can neither pass nor flunk a philosophy test, a guided missile can no more *mis*judge the position of its target than it can correctly perceive it. Psychological descriptions are thus more than mere descriptions; they are also evaluations of behaviour. Suppose, for example, that a psychologist is studying the emotional behaviour of dogs. He gives a dog an electric shock, notes that the dog jumps away from the electrode, and describes the dog's response as 'fear'. Yet motion away from an object is not by itself an adequate criterion of fear. A torpedo repelled by a magnetic field can hardly be described as frightened by it. Moreover, a dog will move away from objects for

motives other than fear – he will avoid objects that bore him or dis-
please him, and even things that attract him, as in the case of the
canine coquette who teases her mate by running away. In order to
identify correctly the particular emotion that motivates the observed
response, as fear, boredom, displeasure or coquetry, the psychologist
must first *evaluate* the stimulus as fearful, or boring, or unpleasant or
tantalising. But such evaluation makes use of normative standards that
happen to be the conventional standards of the psychologist's society,
standards which he projects into the poor dog who is in no position to
complain about the relativity of normative standards. Suppose the dog
were clever enough to talk, and suppose he regarded electric shocks as
rather thrilling: he might advise the psychologist to read Jean-Paul
Sartre before imposing his bourgeois values on canine bohemians.

The essential role of normative judgment in psychological description
makes the deductive model of explanation employed in natural science
inappropriate to psychology. By the deductive model I mean that an
event is explained by deducing it from a set of laws together with
antecedent conditions that we call the 'cause'. Now any so-called law
that might be used as a premise in deducing a psychological event
would have to be phrased in terms that presuppose normative judgments. For example, take the behavioural law: 'Whenever an animal is
confronted by a fearful stimulus, it tries to avoid that stimulus.' How
are we to determine objectively whether a stimulus is fearful? What is
fearful to a coward is not so to a hero; a penthouse apartment is awe-
some to an acrophobe, but delightful to a social climber. The sight of a
rare insect inspires terror in the insectophobe and joy in the entomolo-
gist. The behaviourist might argue that these cultural and idiosyncratic
differences of normative standards among human beings do not apply
to animals, and that for this very reason, animal psychology can be
studied with greater scientific objectivity than human psychology. But
the degree to which this is true is also the degree to which it is pointless
to speak of animal psychology at all, because psychological predicates
like 'fear' no longer do any informative work. It may be true that all
dogs are repelled by just the same stimulus objects. If so, then we
could formulate laws like: 'All canines are repelled by electrically
charged objects.' But notice that the word 'fear' has now dropped out
of the law, since it serves no informative purpose. The reason why we
distinguish *motivating* states like fear, anger, boredom, etc. in describing human behaviour is precisely because human beings do *not* always
respond in the same way to the same stimuli. Concepts like 'fear',
'anger', and 'boredom' serve to explain these differences of response
by indicating the *reasons* why a person avoids an object at one time
and embraces it at another, and such reasons have essential reference
to the normative standards of the agent. Where standards are so
stereotyped that all agents respond to a given stimulus in the same way

(as in the case of avoiding a red-hot stove), psychological intervening variables become vacuous and can be dispensed with altogether. If all human responses were like the automatic response to a hot stove, there would be no need for language that distinguishes human fear from magnetic repulsion or romantic love from gravitational attraction.

The difficulty here has to do with the subtle difference between observable properties of things and criteria of normative judgment. Let us consider this difference briefly:

Any observable property can serve as a criterion or standard of normative judgment, as a result of which it is easy to confuse the mere *presence* of the property with its *role* as a normative standard. For example, a poor man like myself uses mileage and durability as standards for preferring a car or judging it to be good. But the fact that a car is good according to these standards is a fact of a different kind from the fact that it is economical to run. A rich man may regard the car as bad for the very reason the poor man regards it as good, according to Veblen's theory of conspicuous consumption. Thus for the poor man to say that the car is good is not *equivalent* to saying that it is economical to run. For the rich man can agree with him that the car is economical without agreeing that it is good. For the same reason, it is one thing to report that a dog moved away from an electrified object and quite another to say that the dog avoided the object, or that he manifested fear of it; the latter description implies that the dog's response was appropriate to a fearful stimulus, which in turn implies that the stimulus object is in some way bad, or undesirable. Now normative standards are often so conventional and stereotyped that we take the normative judgment as tantamount to an empirical description as when I, as one poor man, say to another poor man that a certain car is a good one. He naturally understands me to be informing him that the car in question is economical and durable. Similarly, when a psychologist reports that a dog feared an electrified object, we take that as tantamount to saying that the dog jumped away from the object, because standards of fearfulness of stimuli like electric shocks and standards of appropriate response are stereotyped among humans as well as dogs. So if we confuse values with empirical facts in such cases, no practical damage is done. But this is true only of very rudimentary situations. Consider, for example, that a boxer often avoids a blow, not by running away from it, but by moving toward it and clinching, which is not a standard fear response. Again, if a person knows that an electric shock will cure him of an illness, or if he has formed an eccentric fascination for electric shocks, the difference between value judgment and empirical fact becomes crucial, since he might embrace the electrode in fear, or move away from it in fascination. If there were canine saints and canine masochists, capable of abstaining from food no matter how hungry they were, the differences between the motives of hunger, duty and self-punishment would be essential to our descriptions of their food behaviour. But if such things as canine saints and canine masochists are excluded as possibilities, then canine psychology is indistinguishable from canine physiology, and psychological descriptions are superfluous restatements of physiological descriptions.

## *Intentionality*

I would like now to consider a third difference between psychological language and physical language, and then I shall try to tie these three distinctions together. Some philosophers have defined psychological terms as those possessing the property of intentionality, where by 'intentionality' they mean a relation between a subject X and an object Y that holds independently of the existence of Y. Thinking, believing, loving, wanting are intentional states in the sense that X can think about, believe in, love or want Y whether Y exists or not. Franz Brentano was the first to emphasise this feature of psychological language, and Roderick Chisholm has made effective use of it in an illuminating critique of behaviouristic psychology.[5]

This peculiar feature of psychological language helps further to explain why psychological inquiry cannot be modelled on inquiry in the natural sciences. If the object of an intentional state like belief or emotion need not exist, then it is impossible to verify sentences about such states by means of observable evidence alone, and it is equally impossible to formulate empirical laws associating such states with observable behaviour. For example, we cannot say that an organism always avoids an *objectively* fearful stimulus, but only that an organism always avoids what *it believes to be* a fearful stimulus, for there may be no external stimulus at all, as in the case of hallucination, or the real stimulus object may be innocuous, as when an animal is frightened by a shadow. Thus concepts like 'fear' and 'avoidance' are intentionally related to objects independently of the real properties and even of the existence of such objects and cannot therefore be operationally defined in terms of observable events alone.

The criterion of intentionality employed above has been criticised for begging questions about the meaning of 'existence' and 'reality', and for being both too broad and too narrow to cover the gamut of psychological discourse. Many plausible counter examples have been offered by W. Sellars, D. Rosenthal, H. Morick, and others. However, whatever the deficiencies of the Brentano–Chisholm criterion, they need not affect our discussion, since all that matters here is that the truth value of some 'crucial' (in a sense explained in Chapter 2) psychological statements be dependent on the beliefs of, or the descriptions acceptable to, the subject of the statement in question. For example (thanks to Fred Dretzke), 'The child saw his father take a stick out of the closet', when used intentionally, becomes false when 'umbrella' is substituted for 'stick', but remains true when used non-intentionally. I am of course employing 'intentional' as a feature of our *use* of sentences, and not as a semantic property of sentences themselves. Perhaps I should say, more precisely, that I am stipulating this meaning of the technical term 'intentionality' for my own purposes.

PSYCHOLOGICAL EXPLANATION

We have considered three features of psychological language that distinguish it from the language of natural science: non-observational self-application, essential reference to normative standards, and intentionality. These three peculiarities have an important bearing on the kind of explanations appropriate to psychology and other behavioural sciences, like sociology, anthropology and history. I want to argue now that explanations of human actions – as contrasted with explanations of organic inability to act – are of a fundamentally different type from explanations of natural phenomena in physics, chemistry and biology.

It is fashionable these days to take the view that all explanations are of the same general nature, a view that was most thoroughly articulated by Ernest Nagel in his monumental study, *The Structure of Science*.[6] Logical empiricists, whose views have been accepted as canonical by many American psychologists, grant that there is a difference between deterministic and probabilistic explanation, that is, between explaining why an event *had* to happen and why it was *likely* to happen, the difference lying in our inability to isolate all the causal factors that determine the event in question. But they recognise no other kinds of explanation than these. According to this view, explanation and prediction have the same logical structure and differ only with respect to whether the event in question is past or future. To explain is to retrodict, to *predict* is to explain in advance. To do either is, essentially, to deduce an event or its probability from antecedent conditions by means of linking generalisations. If the generalisations are statistical, then the explanation is probabilistic; if the generalisations are laws in the sense that they cover all cases, then the explanation is deterministic or strictly causal.

Now it is a notorious fact that there are no non-trivial deterministic laws of psychology or of any other behavioural science. There are, of course, plenty of valuable statistical generalisations about behaviour that help us to predict the probability of individual or group behaviour under well-defined antecedent conditions, but these statistical generalisations are descriptive rather than explanatory. For example, the generalisation that most three-year-old children have temper tantrums enables us to predict that Johnny will (probably) have temper tantrums, but it is obviously not an *explanation* of Johnny's behaviour. What remains to be explained is *why* Johnny and other children of his age have temper tantrums, and this curious fact of life is hardly explained by the generalisation that it usually does happen, nor does it help to add the pseudo-explanation that temper tantrums are a normal stage of ego-development, for this is just a fancy way of repeating the fact to be explained, namely, that three-year-old children usually have temper tantrums.

On the other hand, whether or not there are causal laws of psychology, there certainly are such things as psychological explanations whose adequacy has nothing to do with laws. If, during a game of bridge, Mr Jones gives his wife a kick in the shins and his wife protests, 'Why did you do that to me?' Mr Jones's reply, 'Because you trumped my ace, you idiot!' is a perfectly adequate explanation of his action, although it has nothing to do with prediction, probability or law. It would be absurd to claim that there is any law-like relation between having one's ace trumped and kicking one's partner. Nor is it necessary or even appropriate to look for a statistical probability of such a response to such a stimulus, since it is perfectly conceivable that no one except Jones behaves in this barbaric way. All we need to know, in order to be sure that Mr Jones's explanation of his action is true, is that he is sincere when he gives his reason for it. We must, of course, distinguish avowed reasons from real or motivating reasons, and psychologists are specially trained to spot the differences between genuine motives and mere pretexts. If we note that, when the attractive blonde next door sits opposite Mr Jones and trumps his ace, Mr Jones responds with a sympathetic smile, then we are entitled to suspect that Jones's real reason for kicking his wife was other than his avowed reason. Giving a reason for one's action involves appeal to some rule of conduct, such as 'Players who trump their partners' aces should be punished', and the main test of a person's sincerity in appealing to a rule is his consistency in following it. When Hitler invaded Czechoslovakia ostensibly to protect the rights of German residents there, we know that his alleged reason was not his real motive because he showed no regard for the rights of minorities in his own country nor, for that matter, of German citizens themselves.

These rather crude examples are intended only to illustrate that explaining actions in terms of reasons is a different kind of procedure from explaining natural phenomena in terms of antecedent conditions and laws. Psychological explanations of human actions are couched in terms of concepts like reason, motive, belief, value and intention, concepts that cannot enter into the causal laws and theories of natural science because of the three features I discussed above, namely, non-observational self-ascription, intentionality and dependence on normative standards. Since they cannot enter into the formulation of laws, it is scientifically pointless to construct theories of motivation, for the scientific value of a theory lies in the new laws that can be deduced from the theory. I suggest, therefore, that all causal theories of motivation are products of conceptual confusion between causal and rational explanation. In the remainder of this chapter, I shall try to indicate why psychologists are so often tempted to confuse these two kinds of explanations, and why it is important for them to resist the temptation.

Psychoanalytic theorists sometimes describe human motivation on analogy with an iceberg – one-tenth above the surface and nine-tenths below. But it can be argued on philosophical grounds that the inverse of this analogy is more apt: motivation must be nine-tenths conscious or unproblematic, and only one-tenth or so clandestine and obscure. For, as Sidney Shoemaker has argued in *Self Knowledge and Self Identity*,[7] we could not possibly learn to use the concepts of reason, desire, feeling and intention if this inverse analogy did not hold. We learn to use these concepts primarily in a self-ascriptive way. Piaget describes how small children first employs phrases like 'I want X' as commands or requests, long before they can talk in a purely factual way about what other people want. Thus in order to understand the logic of 'want', we must take note of the fact that 'want' is primarily self-ascriptive, and only derivatively descriptive of others. As self-ascriptive, there are no observable criteria of its application – I need not look at myself in a mirror in order to say 'I want a cup of coffee'. Nor, in ordinary circumstances, need the waitress scrutinise me to see if I really do want coffee. (By 'ordinary circumstances' I mean I am not drunk and I don't look like a hobo or a madman.)

Now, if the primary use of psychological predicates – the use that we learn first – is non-observationally self-ascriptive, then it follows that, under normal circumstances, we must necessarily take a person's description of himself at face value. When I tell a waitress that I want a cup of coffee, she takes my word for it. Taking a person's word for his psychological descriptions of himself is not a privilege we extend to him for good conduct, nor is it a certificate we award him when he has completed 300 hours of psychoanalysis. Rather, it is a logical condition for the meaningful use of psychological language. As Shoemaker puts it, psychological self-ascriptions are necessarily generally true, that is, they *must* be taken as true under standard conditions, where no extraordinary factors conducive to insincerity or self-deception can be found – factors such as delusion, intoxication, extreme fear, having something to gain by lying, etc. But if this is true, then the claim that the larger part of human motivation lies concealed beneath the surface of consciousness must be false, since it contradicts the very condition that distinguishes psychological language from physical language, namely, the condition of privileged authority for one's self-ascriptions, which is the first thing the child learns from his parents about psychological language. Thus, in making the erroneous iceberg claim, psychoanalytic theory has tended to reduce psychological language to physical language. It is true of a physical iceberg that most of it lies beneath the surface of the water, and this is a fact that we can verify by diving underneath and looking. But there is no way to verify what lies beneath a man's consciousness except by so arranging conditions through psychotherapeutic procedures that the abnormal conditions for erroneous self-ascription are transformed into normal conditions for true self-ascription. Psychoanalysis can be regarded in this light as a technique for restoring the standard conditions of psychological self-description. In this respect, psychoanalysis is a more subtle and effective set of procedures, but of the same general type, as giving a drunk a cold shower, reassuring a frightened witness by palliating his fear of public or family criticism, or responding with kindness and patience to a hostile and suspicious child. A. C. MacIntyre has made this point persuasively, in his monograph, *The Unconscious*, in which he argues that, insofar as the concept of unconscious desires and motives has any verifiable sense, it is as an extension of the everyday notion of what we know about ourselves, not at the moment of action, but after calm reflection.[8] Thus the techniques of psychoanalysis presuppose the very principle that psychoanalytic theory denies, namely, that normally we can trust what people say about their own feelings and motives.

But if so, then the difference between a conscious motive and an unconscious motive is not really like the difference between the visible part of an iceberg and the invisible part. It is more like that between knowing a poem that one can recite at will, and knowing a poem that one can piece together only after long and undisturbed efforts at recollection. Unconscious motives are the exception rather than the rule, and we can know they exist only if they become conscious motives when normal conditions of self-description are restored.

All this has an important bearing on the difference between causal explanation and psychological explanation. Freud tended to confuse the two because he thought in terms of something like the iceberg model, with the huge understructure of libidinous motivation constantly exerting a sinister influence on the agent's conduct and thought. Marx thought of social 'dynamics' in a similar fashion, with the substructure of class interests determining political policies, institutions and ideologies. And from these two men of genius we have inherited interesting but scientifically worthless theories of individual and social motivation, according to which, if we know the unconscious substructural forces and laws at work, we can deduce the actions of individuals or groups as a physicist deduces the path of a projectile. The reason why such theories are scientifically useless is that there is no way of identifying the substructural causes except by their effects, that is, by what the person or group says and does. But explanations of this kind are like

Molière's doctor who explained that opium puts one to sleep because it has a dormitive virtue. The explanation is vacuous because the alleged cause is simply a fancy name for the effect it is supposed to explain, and has no further predictive power. Its scientific 'cash value' is zero.

Psychological explanations in terms of reasons or motives are not causal explanations because they have no predictive power other than the mere projection to the future of behaviour patterns already observed in the past. It is natural then, that psychologists who want to regard their discipline as a science on a par with physics, should try to transform psychological explanations into causal explanations. But in addition to the vacuity of this enterprise, it also misses the point of psychological explanation. The value of an explanation in terms of reasons or motives is not that it enables us to predict anything, but that it enables us to *evaluate* the action in question. When I tell you that my reason for extending my arm outside the window of my car is that I was signalling for a left turn, you judge my action differently from the way you did when you thought I was merely exercising my muscles, or showing off by driving with one hand. Thus the very reason why a rational or psychological explanation is not predictively potent, namely that it is a re-description of the action it explains, is also what makes it extremely useful in another way; it reveals the purposive significance of the action from the point of view of the values of the agent and thus enables us to evaluate the action, together with its reasons, as good or bad, wise or foolish, successful or unsuccessful.

If someone slips on a banana skin, we do not ask for his motive. If I extend my left arm in order to signal for a turn, it is silly to ask what caused me to extend my arm. Causal explanation and motivation explanation are mutually exclusive. To visualise reasons and motives as psychic forces analogous to physical stresses and strains is to obscure the crucial difference between psychology and physics. Reasons enable us to judge if actions are right or wrong, intelligent or foolish. Causes enable us to judge that effects are *neither* right nor wrong, but involuntary and unavoidable.

Does all this entail that causal explanation has no role to play in psychology? If what I have said entailed such a consequence, it would hardly be worth a hearing. It is perfectly obvious that psychologists make effective use of causal knowledge in anatomy, biochemistry and neurology to explain *abnormal* behaviour and to restore the necessary conditions for effective human action. It cannot be denied that a large portion of psychology and psychiatry consists in the experimental discovery and application of knowledge of the organic causes of breakdowns and resuscitations of the human animal. But this portion of psychology is psychology only in a rather negative sense; it is knowledge of what prevents effective action, rather than of what motivates effective action. There are thus two kinds of psychotherapy: (1) the branch of medicine that identifies and restores the necessary organic conditions for human action and (2) the kind that tries to influence an already rational agent to promote his own and others' welfare by offering the agent good reasons for socially desirable conduct. It is worth noting, at this point, that Freud once defined psychoanalysis as 're-education'. Now education does not consist in instituting causal factors that guarantee effective action. A student who scored 100 on an exam without even studying, when and only when he swallowed a certain pill, would not deserve credit for scholarly excellence. The chemist who invented the pill would deserve whatever credit was due.

Where all the *organic* conditions for effective human activity are satisfied, behaviour can be influenced for better or for worse only by non-causal procedures such as moral exhortation, inspirational example, reward and punishment, or rational argument. The religious leader, the philosopher, the school teacher and the psychotherapist employ all these methods in varying proportions with a degree of success that depends more on their personal qualities than on their theological, metaphysical, educational or psychoanalytic theories.

# 2 Authority and Freedom to Avow

'Just try, in a real case, to doubt someone else's pain or fear' –
Wittgenstein, *Philosophical Investigations*

' "So you are saying that the word 'pain' really means crying?"
On the contrary: the verbal expression of pain replaces crying and
does not describe it' – Ibid.

It is, I believe, a little-noticed fact that all psychological knowledge is
erected upon a foundation of first-person, present-tense self-descriptions, felicitously named 'avowals' by Gilbert Ryle. The word
'avowals' is extremely apt because such assertions are not ordinary
descriptions of states of affairs; they are semi-performative in nature,[1]
falling somewhere in between the pure performatives brought to light
by Austin, such as 'I promise', 'I do thee wed' and 'I dub thee Sir
Lancelot', and physical self-descriptions such as 'I weigh 150 pounds'.
I intend to show that psychology cannot be a theoretical science like
biology because its data are 'subjective reports' or avowals, and all
apparently more objective psychological knowledge is built upon these
data, thus sharing their subjectivity. Secondarily, I hope to shed new
light on how and why the human animal has free will, despite the
correct Hegelian–Marxist claim that the individual is a nexus of social
relationships.

My general argument for the logical dependence of all psychological
knowledge on avowals is this: There are no purely mental objects,
states, events or processes, as Wittgenstein, Sartre and Ryle have
sufficiently argued (further arguments are offered later, in Chapter 5).
Consequently it cannot be the job of psychological statements to refer
to and describe and nomologically explain such *non*-entities. Insofar as
psychological statements refer to anything, they must refer (but indirectly and vaguely) to bodily states and processes or tendencies to
such. The primary job of such statements is not referential or descriptive; it is to interpret and evaluate the states of agents, the actions
toward which they incline, and the circumstances that determine the
moral or practical significance of such states and actions. I want to
suggest that the origin of evaluations of circumstances, states and
actions is to be found in the normative judgments of the agent as
expressed in his avowals. Without this foundation in avowals, I shall

maintain, more general psychological statements such as 'Jones is neurotic' or 'Smith has leadership qualities' would be unintelligible.

I will first try to clarify the peculiar logic of avowals and then develop the argument sketched above, in tracing their logical relations to psychological generalisations. In so doing, I hope to account for the four features that distinguish psychological discourse from natural science: (1) non-observational self-knowledge, (2) intentionality,[2] (3) normative judgment[3] and (4) rational rather than causal explanation.[4]

TYPES OF SELF-DESCRIPTIONS AND THE ROLE OF AVOWALS

There are at least eight types of psychologically self-descriptive assertions, of which only two are pure avowals (in the sense of 'avowal' I shall try to spell out below). First I wish to try to clarify the connections and the differences between the six or so non-avowal types and the avowal types. All eight may be illustrated by the following sentences (including some sub-types):

1. I am an irritable person (a generalisation).
2. I was (or will be) shocked by his appearance.
3. I see (or saw) a shark in the water.
4. (a) I remember that there was a shark in the water yesterday.
   (b) I remember her face.
   (c) I dreamt of a golden castle with barred windows.
5. (a) I see something blue.
   (b) I see a bluish patch.
6. (a) I feel cold (or angry, or happy).
   (b) I believe in God (or that God exists).
7. (a) I want coffee.
   (b) I intend to get coffee.
8. I am signalling.

It hardly needs argument to achieve agreement that the first five types are importantly distinct from the last three, in that their truth conditions are radically different. Few would dispute that statements of types 1, 2, 3, 4(a) and 5(a) can be verified and falsified by publicly observable evidence, and that a person can assert them mistakenly even when he is sincere and is choosing his words carefully and deftly. Types 4(b), 4(c) and 5(b) are often claimed to be unfalsifiable in the above sense. Whether or not they are, depends, I suspect, on whether they are taken as weak claims to the truth of their propositional content, or considered rather as purely phenomenological reports. Let us take a moment to explore this complication:

Can 'I remember her face' be disconfirmed by inductive evidence? If I say this of a well-known actress and then describe her with woeful inaccuracy (as dark complexioned when in reality she is fair, as brown-eyed although her eyes are blue, etc.), then surely I can be said to be mistaken. It was not *her* face I remembered, but someone else's (my mother's, perhaps?) or perhaps I simply thought I remembered her but I didn't.

But suppose I insist that nonetheless, by golly, I *do* remember her face, not someone else's, even if my memory image of her face does not do naturalistic justice to its model. I maintain against all my critics that I have a distinct memory image of Miss X's face, no matter how Picasso-like distorted it may be, and I can report that image accurately. For example, in reading about Lady Guinevere, I form an image of her and later remember that image even though there is no Lady Guinevere at all for my image to correspond to, if Quine is right versus Meinong. I can truthfully say that I remember the face of my imaginary Lady Guinevere. So long as I am willing to suspend the issue of the public reality of the object of my imagery, my sincere report of my memory image is not subject to challenge. In this sense, there are lots of things we remember whose public correlates may never have existed, or may have existed in a quite different form from the way we remember them. Think of scenes of your childhood, or Marcel Proust's remembrances of things past, of the ghosts and goblins that remain as toys in our psychic attics (or should I say, basements?), figures in our dreams, fictional characters, etc. The ambiguity of realistic versus phenomenological memory reports was noted by Ryle in *The Concept of Mind*.

My point here is that, insofar as there is a phenomenological use of memory reports, the publicly incorrigible character of such reports may be accounted for in a way similar to that of avowals proper (see below), in terms of the authority and freedom of the subject to interpret and evaluate his own immediate state and inclinations. No one but the subject (provided he is clinically normal) has the right and the authority to *decide* what his experience means *to him*. This truism is, I think, semantically entailed by the very concepts of thought, desire, intention and image. So one's so-called phenomenological memory report is less a report than it is an authoritative declaration, resembling, but not identical with, a jury's verdict or an executive's decree.

The same considerations hold of dream reports, and even more strongly so, because, as Malcolm noted there is no ambiguity, or, more accurately, much less ambiguity between realistic and phenomenalistic dream reports (whether, as Malcolm suggests, the former do not exist at all need not concern us here). The experience of remembering a dream and reporting it to oneself or to another is the only waking experience that provides knowledge of the occurrence and content of the dream (setting aside the REM experiments which, as Malcolm shows, beg the very question they attempt to decide experimentally, for what have the psychologists to go on except the subject's report when they wake him up, and how can they check his dream time scale against their real physical watches?). One may be tempted as always to identify the conditions for knowing a fact (i.e. the evidence) with the fact itself, and so to conclude that a dream is just the experience of remembering a dream and that remembering it is identical with sincerely telling it. But such temptations should be resisted. As G. E. Moore noted long ago, in his 'Refutation of Idealism', the experience of phi must be distinguished from phi itself, or else the experience would not be an experience *of* something, and thus not an experience at all. Nor can an experience be of itself on pain of an infinite and vicious regress in defining the concept of experience. Thus the dream remembered and reported is not the remembrance or the report, but it does not follow from this point of logical grammar that a dream must be a real event that occurs in space and time. It may well be that, like mental images, ideas, and all other *soi-disant* 'psychic phenomena', dreams neither take place nor fail to take place, but are simply remembered and reported, just as after images neither exist on the wall nor fail to exist on the wall, but are the sort of things that are simply, as Ryle would say, 'grammatical accusatives' of a certain type of visual experience.

Considering now perceptual reports of types 3 and 5 (a and b), although I have said that perceptual reports are publicly falsifiable, a qualification must be made at this point, in the light of the ambiguities revealed earlier. We *can* use type 3 as a purely phenomenological report (e.g. all right, so there's no shark there, but I know what I saw, and what I saw was a shark with great big teeth, not a dolphin or a log). But such a use is rather infrequent just because it tends to mislead us without the kind of adequate contextual preparation we get, for example, in an optometrist's examination room. As for reports of type 5(a), as Austin has noted, they are ways of hedging against untrustworthy visual conditions, organic or environmental. 5(b) suffers from the ambiguity discussed above, between reporting seeing a real patch, and phenomenologically reporting an experience that may very well be hallucinatory, as when one rubs one's eyeball. Such reports, as Austin put it, are ways of 'refusing to stick our necks out'.

At this point, before we get to pure avowals, I would like to express some reservations about statements of type 6(b). Belief reports, like memory reports and certain perceptual reports, can perhaps be meant in either a strong or a weak sense, i.e. committally or non-committally. 'I believe that the ice is thin', according to Ryle, can be falsified if the speaker shows no fear of skating on the ice. But this is true only if the statement is taken in its fullest practical import, as it usually would be, since belief statements are *usually* made in a context calling for decision and action. But surely this is not always so. There is no semantical or pragmatic anomaly in asserting 'I believe that parachute is safe although you'll never get me to jump with it'. We have a right to avail ourselves of a purely intellectual use of 'I believe' where no commitment to action is intended. The reason why language provides for such non-committal uses of belief declarations is that we sometimes want to know what people are willing to support intellectually (i.e. by evidence), independently of what they are willing to do about it, and this in turn is because willingness to act on a belief involves factors such as habits, skills, self-confidence and whatever hang-ups our psychic flesh is heir to.

AVOWALS PROPER

Now we can proceed to consider the differences between pure avowals of types 6 and 7 and the objectively corrigible self-descriptions of types 1 to 5.

The difference between the phenomenological uses of self-descriptions just considered, and the uses of pure avowals, is this: the former depend logically on realistic use; they are employed as hedging devices, i.e. as ways of avoiding responsibility for implications that follow from realistic claims in situations where, for organic or environmental reasons, one is not in a position to be sure of the truth of his claims. Pure avowals, on the other hand, are not in this way parasitic on realistic claims. Their role is to introduce (I am tempted to say 'create', but that would be too strong) *new facts* by declarational fiat, in somewhat the same way, though not quite the same way, that a jury *makes* a defendant a convicted man by pronouncing 'guilty', or a chief of state, as Stephen Toulmin noted *makes* a bill a law by signing it. Similarly, we pronounce what we experience to be painful or pleasant, we declare our beliefs and intentions, we adopt stances and postures by declaring 'I hate you' or 'I love you', we make decisions by declaring 'I'll have coffee', 'I vote for Smith', and we commend and grade by declaring 'I like X', 'I prefer Y'.

The avowal uses of language are closely related to, but not at all identical with the expressive and imperatival uses. Wittgenstein mistakenly suggested, in his *Investigations*, that avowals are purely expressive, e.g. 'I feel pain' is a verbal substitute for a scream or a groan. But such a view fails to account for the truth content of avowals, as a result of which he falsely concluded that they are neither true nor false, thus not quite freeing himself from his positivistic bondage. Now 'X feels pain' when said by Y and 'I feel pain' when said by X *say the same thing*, yet surely the former is not expressive and, since it is true or false, so must the latter be. Equally, it would not do to equate 'I want coffee' with 'Please give me coffee', since 'X wants coffee' said by Y and 'I want coffee' when said by X *say the same thing*, yet the former is clearly not a command or request.[5] Moreover, one can respond to 'Give me coffee' by saying 'Nothing doing, *nyet*'; one can defy, disobey or refuse the command, but one cannot defy, disobey or refuse 'I want coffee'; one can at best (or worst) disregard it, as waitresses so often do. Finally, the avowal makes essential reference to the speaker as subject, while the command or request does so only as direct or indirect object.

Nevertheless, it seems unlikely that avowals, like commands, would ever be employed were it not for their intended effect on the listener. We normally say, 'I want coffee' in order to get the waitress to give us coffee, or 'I have pain' in order to elicit either sympathy, an anodyne, or perhaps dental surgery. How then do avowals differ from commands, requests and exclamations?

As we have already seen, avowals, unlike their rivals, are true or false. They correspond or fail to correspond to equivalent third-person descriptions. 'Jones has a toothache' when said by Smith and 'I have a toothache' when said by Jones assert the same fact and are true or false together. On the other hand, 'Give me coffee' has no third person descriptive equivalent and is neither true nor false, nor is an expressive cry of pain.

Another difference, related to the above, is that avowals, unlike commands and expressive exclamations, have logical implications. There are semantical and syntactical rules permitting us to infer consequences from avowals. 'I have pain' permits us to infer that the speaker dislikes the state he is in and would, if he could, *ceteris paribus*, initiate some change in his circumstances. These differences naturally tempt us to lump avowals with publicly corrigible self-descriptions like 'I weigh 150 pounds'. But that this temptation should be resisted is clear when we consider the following differences (aside from those already revealed above):

1. In a physical self-description, the first person pronoun 'I' is replaceable by the speaker's name or any unique description of him without change of truth conditions. But this is not the case for genuine avowals. 'I love you' and 'Raziel Abelson loves you', even when said by the person known as Raziel Abelson, do not have quite the same modal conditions.[6] They are not *necessarily* (although they may well be contingently) substitutable *salva veritatis*. For it is a contingent fact that my name is Raziel Abelson. I might have been substituted for another infant when I was born, or I might suffer from amnesia, or I may be pretending to be Abelson whom I have just murdered. Yet if I say *sincerely* 'I love you', it could not pos-

sibly be the case that *I*, whoever I really am, do not feel love for you. At least, it could not possibly be the case that my statement is false due to *any misidentification of the subject of my statement*, of the kind previously indicated.

2. As Anscombe and Strawson have pointed out and shown the great importance of, we are in a privileged position to make true (when sincere) or false (when we have reason to lie) avowals without any need for observational evidence, but this is not the case for physical self-descriptions nor, as we shall see later, for *general* psychological self-descriptions. I know that I weigh 150 pounds on the basis of the same kind of observational evidence (namely, scale readings) by which anyone else could know this fact about me.

The similarities and differences noted between avowals and imperatives and expressive or performative exclamations, on the one hand, and physical self-descriptions on the other, tempt philosophers to assimilate avowals either to the former (Wittgenstein and Austin) or to the latter (classical empiricism and phenomenology). But to serve as data for psychological generalisations, avowals *must* be more objectively informative than imperatives, exclamations, and pure performatives, and they must also be more authoritatively incorrigible than physical self-descriptions or even general psychological self-descriptions. Thus to assimilate them to either side of the subjective–objective divide would deprive them of their distinctive value, which is just to bridge that divide by establishing facts about oneself that no one else can possibly establish (they can only guess, and could not even guess if there were not already the established practice of self-avowal).

One final point on the relation of avowals to performatives: In *How to Do Things with Words*, Austin assimilated avowals to performatives. This suggestion is, I think, as close to being right as it is possible to get while still being wrong. Avowals, like performatives, are unchallengeable by contrary evidence because they are not conclusions from evidence or matters of direct (introspective) observation. Thus it is as silly to say 'You don't really feel pain' as to say, 'You don't really do' (to a bridegroom saying 'I do') unless we mean only to bring attention to features of the situation that produce what Austin calls 'infelicity', namely, that the presupposed conditions that authorise the declaration are in some way at fault (e.g. that the priest at the wedding is really an escaped convict – and he is not Father Berrigan). But unlike performatives, avowals, even when challenged for good cause, such as signs of insincerity or of poor choice of language, *remain authoritative*, if not withdrawn voluntarily by the speaker and if insistently repeated (e.g. I assure you, I swear to you that I really do feel pain, all appearances to the contrary notwithstanding, and I assure you I mean pain and not just discomfort, etc.). We *cannot* deny the

speaker's authority for his avowals, without relegating him to the dust-
bin, if not of history, at least of the normal human community. To do
this is to commit him to an institution for the mentally, morally or
emotionally defective.

A further difference between avowals and performatives is that
unlike avowals, performatives are not true or false statements, but
ceremonialised verbal acts. In this respect, jury verdicts and official
decrees are performatives, but not avowals. To say: 'I promise' is to
do something namely, to promise. To say 'We find the defendant
guilty' is to do something, namely, to convict him. But to say 'I feel
pain' is surely not to feel pain and to say 'I love Sally' is not in itself
to love Sally, although it may help a bit to produce or intensify that
love. The fact asserted is not identical with the act of asserting it,
although they are interestingly linked, as we shall see in a moment.
Thus avowals are challengeable in a way that performatives are not,
namely, as insincere. (A note of caution is needed here about the
ambiguity of 'insincerity'. An act of promising may be said to be
insincere, but not in the same *sense* as that which applies to avowals.
An insincere promise is one that the agent does not intend to keep, but
this fact does not make it any the less a promise – it does not make it
false to assert that he did indeed promise. Quite the contrary. But the
insincerity of 'I love you' does make it false for the speaker to say
what he said.)

Yet despite these important differences, avowals and performatives
are closely related because they perform similar linguistic jobs of
establishing facts by verbal means. In the case of performatives, the
fact established is the utterance itself, while in the case of avowals,
the fact avowed is not the avowal of it. Nonetheless, the avowal, like the
performative, is logically connected with what it asserts, although the
logical connection is considerably weaker. Under normal conditions,
the sincere avowal is logically *sufficient* for its own truth, *but not
logically necessary*, while a performative is logically both necessary and
sufficient, not for its own truth, since it has no truth value, but for
performing successfully the task for which it is designed, such as
promising, marrying, authorising, etc. provided of course that the presupposed institutional conditions are satisfied. It is because of their
logical sufficiency for what they assert that both types of utterances are
unchallengeable as honestly false. And this logical sufficiency is their
very function for the following reason:

We leave it to the agent what to make of the state he is in, whether
to interpret it as love, as hatred, as pleasure, as pain, etc. We leave it
up to him to decide these matters, as we leave it up to him to decide to
promise, to choose, to authorise officially and to wed. Through avowals
and performatives, one asserts his freedom and his rights as a person,
and any decent society respects those rights and grants that freedom.[7]

We grant these privileges to no other creatures on earth, not even to the very best robots. In this respect, Marx and Hegel were right, that the individual as a free agent is created by society, and Rousseau and Kierkegaard were wrong.

I have used the word 'privilege'. Are avowals and performatives really exercises of privileges? Clearly performatives are. One cannot promise or marry except within a framework of social conventions and mutual trust in which, like a credit card, one's privilege is respected by others unless and until he has so abused the privilege by dishonesty that it is taken away from him. But similarly we cannot avow pain or love or belief to behavioural psychologists who refuse us such privileged authority by taking our utterances as mere 'verbal data', to be explained but not to be believed, just as we ordinary humans would do with a robot.

Now why do we grant these cognitive privileges – why does our language provide for avowals and performatives? The reason lies, I think, in our respect for and our social power to grant individual freedom and authority, by which I mean the following:

We sometimes choose, act and react in ways that could not have been expected even on the basis of considerable knowledge of our past behaviour, habits, culture, etc. Our assumption that we can understand each other presupposes that we have values and goals in common but we also assume that each person arrives at his own unique balance among conflicts and priorities of values. Without this latter assumption, we need never consult him as to his wants and needs, nor need he consult us. Democracy is the institutional recognition that each individual has a unique value system, capable of creative variation at any moment. Democracy is thus the only mode of social organisation that reflects consistently the metaphysical–ethical concept of a person. To be a person is to have the right to normative authority, as Kant first noted. If we all aimed at the same goals to the same degree, like rats in a maze, there would be no need for avowals, as is the case in the society envisioned (naturally) by B. F. Skinner in *Walden II*. Like Kierkegaard *vis-à-vis* Hegel, I wouldn't want to be a robot resident of Skinner's behaviouristic paradise.

AVOWALS AND PSYCHOLOGICAL GENERALISATIONS

I will offer, first, an *a priori* argument to show that general psychological statements are logically dependent on avowals, in that their meaning must be unpacked partially in terms of avowals. Next, I will offer an illustration of the form that such explications might take.

## The A-Priori *Argument*

Assuming, as it seems to me reasonable to do, that psychological language is indispensable for communicating facts that cannot be adequately described in physical language alone, it would seem to follow that psychological concepts must be defined in terms of avowals (not exclusively, but at least in part). For one of the features that makes psychological concepts irreducible to physical concepts is the fact that they can be self-ascribed without observation and this non-observational self-knowledge is precisely, as we have seen, what avowals are designed to convey. Any apparently psychological description of a computer or a robot can be translated without remainder into a physical description. For example, 'The computer became neurotic' translates into 'The computer had a short circuit', or, perhaps, 'A card was inserted involving division by zero, and the effect was circuit hyperactivity and breakdown'. 'The robot is angry' could be translated into some Rylean dispositional formula such as 'If anything approaches it, it will swing a hammer in that entity's direction'. The reason why psychological descriptions of human beings are indispensable (setting aside animal pets who are describable on analogy with humans) is that the human agent can avow his own states without observation and we normally take his word about them. Try, for example, doing social psychology or clinical psychology without avowal-eliciting questionnaires or therapeutic sessions. This is what makes the agent's psychological states irreducible to physical states, since the latter cannot be known without observation; no person or object is granted privileged authority about his physical states.

## The Relation of Generalisations to Avowals

But just what *is* the logical relation between general psychological statements and avowals? It is to be expected that the exact relation would vary from one type of statement to another, depending on the psychological predicate involved, and also on possible ambiguities of sense, such as we noticed earlier with respect to realistic–phenomenological ambiguity, and also the ambiguity of the concepts of sincerity and belief.

Thus I will not attempt to explicate all psychological concepts, not even to provide a complete analysis of a single one. It should be enough, for the purpose of illustrating the logical relations I have referred to with admitted, but inescapable vagueness, to sketch a partial explication of a single psychological generalisation, whereby its logical dependence on avowals is brought to light.

Consider the statement 'John loves Jane'. What kinds of facts are entailed by this statement?

Note first that the explication of meaning in terms of what entails or is entailed by a statement is not the same as the question of evidence, i.e. of what facts, signs or symptoms lead us to conclude, or serve us to confirm that John indeed does love Jane. This latter question can be answered adequately by observing John's behaviour, but not so for the question of criteria, or meaning implications. Suppose that John is a deaf mute, unable to avow his feelings verbally, and ignorant of sign language. Suppose too that when he sees Jane, his eyes brighten, his lips become moist, and his pulse quickens. He seizes every opportunity to perform errands for her, strikes everyone who mistreats her, and looks depressed when she flirts with other men. It would be quite unreasonable to doubt that John loves Jane, despite his inability to avow his feelings.

So far, behaviourism seems correct in claiming that observable evidence is sufficient to establish and confirm the psychological state of love. Or, in a more sophisticated view like that of J. Fodor,[8] at least the evidence establishes an overwhelming probability of the state of love as a hypothetical construct like magnetic lines of force or gravitational attraction. Yet surely, if we are convinced that John loves Jane, as we have every right to be, on the basis of observable evidence alone *in this particular case*, this innocuous fact in no way precludes that, *if* John were able to talk to a confidante, he *would* avow his love for Jane (and, were he not too shy, he would avow it to Jane herself). Now what if John learns sign language and communicates with a trusted friend, and denies to his friend in all sincerity that he loves Jane? We would probably conclude that John is nevertheless in love with Jane but doesn't realise it, represses it; in a word, deceives himself. Again, behaviourism and/or theoretical-hypothetical-construct psychology seems to win the day.

But now consider whether this case could conceivably be generalised as typical. Is it conceivable that we could have such adequate behavioural evidence of the state of love *had we never established a language of avowals*, or were we to abandon it in the future, as Richard Rorty has suggested we very well may? Could we, in such a case, still have a concept of love distinguishable from the concept of a disposition to behave in certain ways, striking out on some occasions, smiling on others, etc.? That is, would we have a concept of love as an emotional state *of which a robot is incapable*, and which is therefore not reducible to purely physical description? Note first that, if we did, it could still not be as rich a concept as it is now, for the very distinction employed above between love of which one is aware and unconscious love would make no sense at all, since the only criterion of *awareness*, namely, ability to avow one's state, would be unavailable.[9]

Nor, on further reflection, could we even have an impoverished concept of love that is any richer than a concept of a tendency, and thus there would be no point to the concept at all. For there would be no way to distinguish the disposition, say, to do favours out of love from that of doing favours out of kindness, or the hope for future reward, or even inverted hostility, since we could not learn to distinguish these motives by comparing the behaviour of others with their avowals, and with our own behaviour and avowals when we are in states whose nature we can know and thus avow without self-observation. It might be countered that we can distinguish the various motives for patterns of behaviour by the goals toward which such behaviour is directed, but first, how could we distinguish the goal *aimed at* from that merely arrived at, without the help either of the agent's avowals, or, assuming him to be like us, without our own avowable non-observational self-knowledge? (And we learn what our own state is when, as small children, we imitate the avowals of our parents.) And secondly, how many goals of human action are observable? Precious few, I should guess; in fact, we should all hope so, because we want to grow, and that means we raise our sights at new goals, and also because the higher, spiritual goals of man are not definable in the language of natural science.

INCORRIGIBILITY

The 'incorrigibility thesis', that full-fledged avowals are normally not subject to challenge (where by 'normal' is meant that the subject is not infantile, is in his right mind, knows the meanings of the words he uses and has no discernible motive to lie), has been severely challenged by science-oriented philosophers, most notably by Richard Rorty in a very influential essay, 'Mind-Body Identity, Privacy and Categories'. It will be instructive to examine Rorty's arguments to see how and why this challenge goes awry, even in the best of hands. Rorty maintains that psychological predicates like 'pain' are, in principle, eliminable from language and with them, the status of 'privacy' (i.e. incorrigibility) that distinguishes them from non-psychological predicates, in somewhat the way that references to witches and demons have been eliminated in favour of psychiatric diagnoses such as that of hallucinatory psychosis, and also in the way that we might someday cease to talk about tables and talk rather about clouds of molecules. His first analogy is nicely provocative, but it is the second that he stresses. Rorty observes that witches and demons are non-observable, explanatory entities that have been replaced by the explanatory entities of psychiatry, while tables are directly observable entities for which we have, as yet, no adequate observable replacements. Consequently 'although we could in *principle* drop "table", it would be monstrously inconvenient to do so, whereas it is both possible in principle and convenient in practice to drop "demon"'. Rorty concludes that although it would be equally inconvenient to drop 'X has pain' in favour of the neurological statement 'X's C-fibres are stimulated', the advance of neurology and encephalography may well result in our being able to observe directly that someone's C-fibres are stimulated, and thus to drop references to pain as we have dropped references to demons, and *could* drop references to tables. The dispensability of psychological self-reports about pain, etc. would become clear when such self-reports are found to be overridden by their neurological equivalents so that their privacy or authority has been undermined. How would this come about? Rorty describes a test-case in the future, as follows:

> The interesting case is the one in which . . . somebody (call him Jones) thinks he has no pain, but the encephalograph says that the brain-process correlated with pain did occur . . .
>
> . . . suppose that Jones was not burned prior to the time that he hitches on the encephalograph, but now he is. When he is, the encephalograph says that the brain-process constantly correlated with pain-reports occurs in Jones' brain. However, *although he exhibits pain behaviour*, Jones thinks that he does not feel pain [my italics, R.A.]. (But now as in the past, he both exhibits pain behaviour and thinks that he feels pain when he is frozen, stuck, struck, racked, etc.) Now is it that he does not know that pain covers what you feel when you are burned as well as what you feel when you are stuck, struck, etc.? . . . The only device which would decide this question would be to establish a convention that anyone who sincerely denied that he felt a pain while exhibiting pain behaviour and being burned *ipso facto* did not understand how to use 'pain'.
>
> . . . We now see that the claim that 'such a mistake is inconceivable' is an ellipsis for the claim that a mistake, made by one who knows what pain is, is inconceivable . . . But when formulated in this way our infallibility about pains can be seen to be empty.[10]

Before I point out Rorty's main mistake, I shall make two preliminary comments: (1) The eliminability of 'table' in favour of 'cloud of molecules' in no way helps to show that an entire *type* of observables is replaceable by theoretical expressions, since 'cloud' is as much the name of an observable as 'table'. And if one tries to replace 'cloud' by some purely theoretical term, what will do the job? 'Swarm', 'collection', 'bunch', 'congeries', 'crowd'? All these are names of observables, unless used metaphorically. Obvious as this point is, it seems not obvious enough to those who have such faith in theoretical language as to believe that our only reason for our non-technical vocabulary is 'pragmatic convenience'. (2) Unlike 'table', 'pain' does an expressive and evaluative job, as Wittgenstein has pointed out.[11]

That is *why* 'I have pain' is incorrigible. When I say that I have pain, I do more than report a fact – I plead for assistance and express my abhorrence for the state I am in and my desire to escape it. If some day we were to employ expressions like 'My C-fibres are stimulated' to do this expressive–evaluative job, then such assertions made in the first-person present indicative would have been recruited *to do the same job* as 'I have pain', and would thus have acquired a psychological meaning (use). In such case, 'My C-fibres are stimulated' would no longer function as a neurological report and it would no longer be corrigible by public criteria such as encephalograph readings. When I then say, 'My C-fibres are stimulated', and you reply, 'Not at all, the encephalograph shows no such indication', I would be entitled to reply: 'Never mind the encephalograph; I know when I want assistance, and when I don't like the state I'm in!' You then have two choices: you can disregard *how I feel*, concerning yourself only with the scientifically provable facts, in which case you have removed yourself from the moral community of persons who care about how others feel, or you will respond to me in just the way you would if I said that I have pain. The economy achieved by replacing 'I have pain' with 'My C-fibres are stimulated' would be merely terminological. The language game of authoritative avowals cannot be dispensed with, unless we are prepared to dispense with that democratic respect for the evaluations of persons on which the equality of individual rights and interests depends. As Wittgenstein and Strawson have put it, to accept the avowals of others as authoritative is to *see* them as persons, rather than as automata.

The most serious mistake in Rorty's argument consists in what appears at first sight to be a minor slip. In his account of his imaginary experiment of the future, in which an encephalograph reading over-rides a pain-avowal, Rorty supposes that Jones exhibits pain behaviour, but denies sincerely that he feels pain. Now what exactly *is* pain behaviour? Presumably, groaning, twitching and attempting to escape what one takes to be the source of pain (in Rorty's example, a hot object). Why do we call such gestures and actions 'pain behaviour'? Is it not because, as Wittgenstein observed, they are natural *expressions* of pain, not merely contingent effects, but part of what 'pain' entails, so that someone who groans and twitches is letting us know that he is in pain? If he then says he is not in pain, either he is lying (which Rorty rules out *ex hypothesi*) or else *of course* he shows inadequate misunderstanding of the meaning of 'pain'. But this has nothing to do with the encephalograph indication that his C-fibres are stimulated. It has rather to do with the inconsistency of his natural expressions of pain and his verbal expression. To claim corrigibility of a pain avowal in such a case is to win an empty victory, since it is not the *encephalograph* that is overriding Jones' denial of pain, it is his own gestural expressions of pain. The appropriate test-case for Rorty's corrigibility thesis would be one in which all of Jones' expressions, both gestural and verbal, were consistent, e.g. he smiles, welcomes being burned again, and says he enjoys it, although the encephalograph registers that his C-fibres are firing. In *that* case we should say 'So much the worse for the neurological theory that the firing of C-fibres is necessary and sufficient for pain.'

It was surely a slip on Rorty's part to stack the cards in favour of his corrigibility thesis by postulating pain *behaviour* in support of the encephalograph reading he wished to make authoritative. But it was a very revealing slip, for it shows how easily one can shift from psychologically significant behaviour to mere bodily movement, assume that nothing has been lost, and thus 'prove' that psychology is reducible to biology or physics. What we call 'pain behaviour' is not mere bodily movement; it is movement that *expresses* what we feel, and thus 'tells' others what we feel. In the way a groan or a twitch cannot be mistaken, but only insincere, 'I have pain' cannot be mistaken, but only insincere. It is true that 'I have pain' can be not only insincere, but also false, while a groan cannot be false, and this is so because 'I have pain' is *both* an expressive utterance *and* a report of a fact, the fact that I feel pain. Nevertheless, it is a report of a fact about which one cannot be honestly mistaken. It may well be that this fact can be explained neurologically, but the explanation cannot substitute for 'I have pain' because 'I have pain' is more than a pain report, it is also an *expression* of pain – thus itself a mode of pain behaviour.

The general thesis I have argued for is that avowals are our primary criteria for identifying each other's immediate psychological states, and even our own long-term psychological tendencies (which are tendencies to get into the immediate states such as anger, pain, etc. that become known to others through our avowals primarily, and our behaviour secondarily). Behavioural criteria and symptoms, while often adequate *within a conceptual framework based upon avowals*, become hopelessly impoverished when deprived of that framework. And the reason for this is that avowals are our unique way of making public the states of which we have non-observational self-knowledge, the reason in turn for which is that human social evolution, in creating a language of avowals and institutions within which it can be effectively employed, has made us free and creative individuals.

# 3 Cause and Reason

> 'But why do you say that we felt a causal connexion? ... One might
> rather say, I feel that the letters are the *reason* why I read such-and-
> such. For if someone asks me "Why do you read such-and-such?" –
> I justify my reading by the letters which are there' – Wittgenstein,
> *Philosophical Investigations*

Having found, in avowals and performatives, an irruption into the
natural world by human agents that must be incompletely determined,
if its author is to have incorrigible authority, the question arises: does
this entail that human *actions* are causally undetermined as well, and,
if so, are they therefore inexplicable?[1] Our answer to the first question
will be affirmative and our answer to the second negative. I suspect
that the aversion most philosophers have to indeterminism is due to
their mistaken fear that it entails an affirmative answer to the second
question. I shall try to allay that fear.

So far we have considered only verbal actions, and of these, only a
subset: avowals and performatives. We must now consider the logical
relation, if any, between such speech acts and overt bodily actions in
order to decide if the causal indeterminism of the former affects the
latter. I believe it does.

I shall argue that voluntary human actions of any kind, verbal or
non-verbal, are not explainable by causes, not insofar as they logically
could have causes though in fact they lack them, but in the stronger
sense that either to affirm causes of actions or to deny causes of actions
is semantically anomalous, amounting to what Ryle has called a
'category mistake'. We have already considered why this claim holds
for avowals and performative speech acts. I now want to show, with
regard to non-verbal (voluntary) actions, that an adequate explanation
of such actions involves avowals as part of the *explanans*, so that the
indeterminism of the latter entails the indeterminism of the former.

The explanation of a voluntary action always, I maintain, involves
reference to the agent's avowals because actions are explained in terms
of *reasons*, and an agent's reasons can only be known – indeed, can
only come into existence – through his avowals. Reasons are appeals
by a litigant to premises of an argumentative conclusion, in justification or exculpation of what he says or does, and the litigant is the final
authority, having authoritative non-observational self-knowledge, on

what his reasons are. It is for him to select the grounds on which he rests his case, grounds that manifest his choices of relative values and priorities, that is, of what *for him* constitutes adequate justification or exculpation. Insofar as we share his values we will find his reasons to be good reasons; to the degree that our own priorities differ from his, we may judge his reasons to be bad. If we differ too radically, we may be unable to see his reasons as even bad reasons, and we will consider him so irrational as to be unable to make authoritative avowals; in a word, insane.

The argument for this view leads us back to Ryle's *Concept of Mind* and the conceptual revolution which he and Wittgenstein began.

THE CONCEPTUAL REVOLUTION

Gilbert Ryle's *The Concept of Mind* charted a new direction for studies in philosophical psychology. Ryle's explicit aim was to demolish Cartesian dualism and its privileged access criterion of mind. In performing this demolition job, he also accomplished something positive. Intentionally or not, Ryle forged a new kind of dualism in the ashes of the old. In arguing that mind and matter are not different kinds of substances, Ryle revealed that mental and physical concepts are radically different kinds of concepts. Metaphysical dualism gave way to conceptual dualism.

But Ryle did not follow out the implications of his new dualism as far as they promise to lead. Others have done that since. Toulmin, Nowell-Smith, Hare, Mayo and Baier have deepened our understanding of the difference between normative and descriptive discourse, while Austin, Peters, Urmson, Anscombe, Hamlyn, Dray, Melden, and C. Taylor have discovered new categorial boundaries separating psychological concepts such as motivation, belief, perception, intention and volition from the language of natural events and processes. I think there is a good reason why the impact of *The Concept of Mind* on both ethics and psychology was equally great. The most important result of Ryle's attack on metaphysical dualism – a result which, for a reason that I shall try to explain below, Ryle himself did not fully appreciate – was the increasing realisation that the purposive language in which we talk about human conduct is inescapably normative, and that psychology and sociology are logically dependent on ethics, rather than the other way round. R. Peters, in *Motivation*, and P. Winch, in *The Idea of a Social Science*, have brought these implications to light.

In his chapter on emotion in *The Concept of Mind* Ryle offered a dispositional analysis of affective states such as emotion and desire, according to which they turn out not to be internal states at all, but to be 'reasons' for predicting vague ranges of overt behaviour. Emotions

as motives, Ryle contended, are not inner springs of action; they are
reasons for our acts, not causes of our acts.[2] But Ryle failed to note
the categorial gap between reasons and causes which his own analysis
should have suggested to him. He assumed that reasons and causes
work together in the same type of explanation. The cause of an event
or action is, for Ryle, some antecedent event or stimulus, while the
'reason' is a law-like conditional generalisation, licensing us to infer
the occurrence of the effect or response.[3] Ryle thus remained a scientific
determinist on the issue of free action, while dissociating himself from
mechanistic behaviourism and from mind–body dualism. What he
failed to see, and what Peters, Dray and Melden have since brought to
light, is that the concept of cause (in its natural scientific sense) cannot
intelligibly be applied to the explanation of human action. For three
centuries philosophers have been purging natural science of purposive
language. The ill-fitting shoe is now on the other foot and we face the
converse task of expunging pseudo-mechanistic concepts from the
purposive language of human affairs.

CAUSES AND REASONS

Ryle began this task by distinguishing reasons and motives from causes.
But his distinction did not cut deep enough. He recognised that psychological concepts are explanatory rather than referential, but he failed
to see that a psychological explanation is not a causal explanation –
that, in fact, the two are logically incompatible. To cite the motive for
an act and to cite the cause of an event is, in either case, to answer the
question 'Why', but the meaning of the question is different in the two
cases. Dray, Peters and Melden have since revealed fundamental
differences between psychological and causal explanation. They have
argued that to ask 'Why' about a human action is to ask to make the
action intelligible by filling out its purposive context, including the
beliefs and attitudes of the agent who performs it. According to Dray,
a motive is in one way more like a cause than Ryle realised. It is not a
ghostly event, but neither is it a law-like conditional. A motive does
not tell us how the agent *generally* behaves, but rather explains an
action by identifying the agent's reason for doing it. Dray is willing to
grant determinists that a reason may be a special kind of cause.[4] He
argues against Ryle that reasons, like causes, have explanatory power,
while conditional generalisations do not. But a reason for him, is not a
cause in the sense of an antecedent event, and it is not logically linked
to its 'effect' by covering laws.

    A. I. Melden's analysis of the difference between reasons and causes
is both more radical and more consistent than that of either Ryle or
Dray. Melden maintains that the rational explanation of an action is

incompatible with any causal explanation. To ask, 'Why did X perform that action?' is to imply that X's behaviour can be described only in purposive language. Conversely, to ask for the cause of X's behaviour is to imply that X's behaviour was involuntary and that purposive explanation is inappropriate. 'Why did X raise his arm?' asks for the reason. 'What made X's arm rise?' asks for the cause.

Melden offers two main reasons why a rational or purposive explanation is incompatible with a causal explanation: (1) Because the motive for a voluntary action logically presupposes the action it motivates, while a cause must be identifiable independently of its effect.[5] (2) Because the motive of an action is part of the way in which we identify the action. 'As motive it . . . tells us what the person was doing.'[6] For example, raising one's arm in order to signal is a different action from raising one's arm in order to restore circulation.

Melden's arguments are not entirely satisfactory, however, because his first reason is inconsistent with his second reason. If the motive helps to define the action, then it cannot presuppose the action, or else our method of identifying both would be viciously circular. For we must then know the motive in order to identify the action and also know the action in order to identify the motive.

I think Melden's first argument is sound, and that his second argument is wrong. But the proof that his second argument is wrong will provide us with still another reason for agreeing with Melden's thesis that a motive cannot be a cause. The proof I have in mind starts from Melden's first claim, that a motive can only be identified in terms of the action it motivates. It follows from this that it makes no sense to speak of a person's motive *before he has performed the action.* A motive can only be known *ex post facto,* which may explain why psychologists have so much trouble predicting what their patients will do. This consequence of Melden's first argument is independently supported by the facts of language. It would be absurd for a detective to say that Smith's motive for killing Brown was jealousy, if in fact Smith has not killed Brown. (It may be objected that we sometimes do say such things as 'Several people had a motive for the crime', so that the motive seems to exist independently of the action. But here I think it is clear that 'several people had a motive' means the same as 'several people had a *possible* motive' – in other words, a strong, but not decisive reason. We occasionally make the word 'motive' do the same job as the word 'reason', but in such cases it is not doing its own distinctive job of signifying a *motivating* reason.)

Melden is therefore right in maintaining that a motive, in the strict sense of the term, must be identified in terms of the action it has motivated. But if he is right in this, then it must be inappropriate to identify an action in terms of its motive. And there is independent evidence that Melden's second argument is unsound. A man's action can have all sorts of motives; it cannot therefore be uniquely identified by any one of them. Melden argues that a person's motive for raising his arm – say, in order to signal – tells us what he was doing, namely, that he was signalling. But I think that Melden is here confusing what one is *trying* to accomplish with what one is actually doing. Usually these two things coincide and so it is not necessary to distinguish them. But sometimes one tries to signal and fails, in which case, one is not signalling, but merely raising one's arm ineffectually. The point is that we can describe actions in two different ways. We can identify an action by what is actually accomplished, whether the result was intended or not, and we can identify it as a successful or unsuccessful attempt to accomplish some purpose. We can say that a hunter shot his friend by mistake, or we can say that he tried unsuccessfully to shoot a bear with consequences disastrous for his hunting companion. Now these two modes of identification are not on the same level. The first mode is simpler and logically prior to the second. As Melden himself points out, following Ryle, the concepts of successful and unsuccessful effort are logically dependent on the simpler concept of purposive action in paradigmatic situations (such as a healthy man raising his arm) in which the question of success or failure does not arise. You could never teach a child the meaning of failure (or success) unless he first understands what is involved in just doing something. As Ryle has put it, trying, succeeding and failing are 'second order performances', logically parasitic on the first order performance of just plain *doing*.

Setting aside the individual variations, for the moment, and considering the Dray–Peters–Melden theory of psychological explanation as a general insistence on distinguishing reasons from causes, this view suffers from one apparently serious defect. It seems to lead to the ethically unacceptable principle that every action is justifiable; *tout comprendre, c'est tout justifier*. The causal model of psychological explanation, which the Dray–Peters–Melden view is intended to supplant, has always suffered from a similar defect. The causal model makes every action *excusable* in that, given the antecedent conditions of an action, it is assumed that it is not within the agent's power to refrain from the action. From this standpoint human action is not subject to moral evaluation because it is *never* rational. But if we follow Dray's analysis of rational explanation, human action, when fully understood, is *always* rational and therefore always 'the thing to have done'. For if, as Dray claims, the function of explanation by reasons is to make the agent's conduct rationally intelligible and if 'intelligibility' means, as Dray seems to hold, that we can imagine ourselves doing the same thing for the same reasons, then we can never say that the agent was wrong to do what he did. 'All reasons', says Dray, 'must be *good* reasons . . . in the sense that *if* the situation had been as the agent envisaged it . . . then what was done would have been the thing to have done.'[7] This assertion of Dray looks like a *reductio ad absurdum* of his theory of psychological explanation. Only the most tender-hearted social worker would agree that understanding a person's motives requires us to approve of what he does.

Melden, too, seems to equate intelligibility with reasonableness or justifiability. An explanation of an action in terms of its motive or intention, he says, 'reveals an order or pattern in the proceedings'.[8] 'To say of ... a person that he is mad is to write off (his) action as unintelligible.'[9] Psychotic behaviour then is not intelligible behaviour and cannot be explained in terms of motives or reasons. Conversely, it would seem to follow that all actions that *can* be so explained are the reasonable thing to do under the circumstances as envisaged by the agent.

Richard Peters tries harder than Dray and Melden to make a clear enough distinction between justifying an action by good reasons and explaining an action by its motive, so as to avoid the absurd consequences that all psychological explanations are justifications. But Peters's distinction is not sharp enough to do the job. Peters defines a motive as that type of reason which is called for when conduct is: (1) unconventional or non-rule-following, (2) directed toward a goal, and (3) the actual or operative reason why the agent acts as he does.[10] Unfortunately Peters fails to explain just how we can tell which of a number of possible reasons for a person's action is the operative one that satisfies condition (3). The trouble is that Peters, like Dray, Melden, Anscombe, P. Foot, R. Taylor and many others, fails to appreciate the fundamental correctness of Ryle's claim that motives are bound up with character. Peters consequently rules out the only empirical means for judging whether an alleged reason is an operative one or not.

Suppose a hunter shoots his companion instead of the bear he claims to have aimed at. How do we know that he was really aiming at the bear and not at his friend? We must, of course, look first for the pattern of the events and actions surrounding the shooting, e.g. how far from his victim the hunter was standing, how the hunter behaved before and after the fatal shot, etc. But suppose an investigation reveals nothing suspicious about these immediate circumstances while, on the other hand, the investigating detective learns that the victim has been carrying on an affair with the hunter's wife. Wouldn't the detective then have to make an assessment of the suspect's character in order to decide between an innocent and a guilty motive for his action? Peters and Melden make the mistake of considering only the cases where an agent's intention is sufficiently obvious from the immediate context of the act to be unproblematic. But in cases where the motive is in doubt, we must widen the context of inquiry and thereby relate the action to deeper or more permanent traits of the agent.

Despite these difficulties, I think the Dray–Peters–Melden theory of psychological explanation is substantially correct. It needs only to be qualified so that psychological explanation can be clearly distinguished from ethical justification. Closer attention to the difference between real or motivating reasons and merely possible reasons will, I think, allow us to combine the characteriological analysis of Ryle with the empathetic approach of Dray.

Dray thinks of reasons as grounds for justification and he assimilates motives to reasons. Ryle thinks of reasons as character traits and he thereby assimilates reasons to motives. But reasons that are not motives have no psychological reality. They are merely statements to which we appeal in urging or supporting an action in advance (whether to ourselves or to others) and in justifying or excusing an action in retrospect. Reasons are logical appeals made by an appellant to a judge, even when appellant and judge are the same person. As such, they have no empirical relation to observed behaviour and thus no *explanatory* function. To *explain* an action, rather than to support it or justify it, a reason must, as Peters notes, be the agent's *real* reason; it must actually motivate the action. It is this difference between mere reasons and real reasons or motives that tempts us to accept a causal mode of psychological explanation. We tend to assume that the sense of 'real' here involved is that of spatio-temporal occurrence, as if a real reason were an event of some kind. But there is an alternative and, I think, more illuminating way of distinguishing real reasons from merely possible reasons. Why not consider motives to be a special type of reasons, namely, those to which a person could (and, in his candid moments, would) *consistently* appeal in attempting to justify his actions? My real reason or motive for my action is the reason that relates it to other actions of mine in a wider context. If I donate money to charity only when my name is made public, then my avowed reason, 'to help the needy', although it does serve to justify my action, is not my real reason because it is inconsistent with my refusal of funds when the names of donors are not announced. My reasons are not, as Melden claims, patterns of my behaviour. They are whatever statements I make in support of my action. But their reality as motives is, indeed, verified in terms of the observable pattern of my behaviour. Once we distinguish real reasons from justifying but merely possible reasons, it becomes evident that not all real reasons need be good reasons, and that psychological explanation does not entail empathetic justification.[11]

If we make this distinction between reasons and motives, we need not go as far as Dray in holding that understanding a person's action requires us to imagine ourselves doing the same thing under the same circumstances. After all, psychiatrists sometimes succeed in understanding a psychotic patient whose behaviour is irrational from any standpoint. It places too great a strain on the imagination of the psychiatrist to demand that he share, even vicariously, the delusions of his patient. Surely it is sufficient for him to disclose motives for his patient's actions that enable him to predict future outbursts of irrationality. Yet, if motives are reasons and not causes, then how can they be grounds for prediction? I think the answer is that in discovering the motives (real reasons) of a person one has, in effect, disclosed his standards of value – his likes, preferences, aspirations and measures of importance – and one may reasonably assume that he will apply the same standards of value in the future as he did in the past. Scientific studies of human behaviour can thus make reliable inductive inferences from past values and actions to future values and actions without employing explanatory theories based on a causal model.[12]

Thus understanding a person's behaviour does not require us either to see it as causally determined or to find *good* reasons for it; we need only find the *real* reasons for it. An action may be explicable by bad or even absurd reasons, if these happen to be characteristic of the agent. It would take a superhuman effort of the imagination to see how testing one's freedom of action could be a *good* reason for killing a man, although it was Lafcadio's reason in Gide's novel, and it is a major factor in the motivation of juvenile delinquents. Dray's principle that a reason must be good to be intelligible is plausible only insofar as it is misleadingly trivial. Any reason by which a person is motivated is a good reason *for him* in the sense that he *thinks* it is good. But this truism constrains us neither to agree that it is good nor to imagine ourselves mistakenly thinking it to be good.

To give a good reason for an action is to justify it; to give the agent's real reason or motive is to explain it. But it must be granted Dray that there is a logical relation between rational explanation and justification. The motive by which we explain a person's action is the reason to which he could consistently appeal in supporting, urging or justifying actions *to himself* or his confidante. 'In *his* book' his motive justifies, but 'in our book' it need only explain.

Yet even if the point be granted that what we want of a psychological explanation is the reason for the act, and not the cause, may it still not be the case that, since every human act is an event which can be described in physical language, as a certain set of bodily movements, rational explanation and causal explanation, while belonging to different modes of discourse, are yet equally applicable to the same entities, depending on how they are described and what we want to know about them? May not the two kinds of explanation be compatible and of equal value, each in its own way – psychological, when our purpose is to evaluate the action as right or prudent or at least excusable, or the reverse, and physical, when our purpose is to set the bodily movements in their appropriate place in the law-like system of nature? In order to show that the answer to this question is negative, I shall examine the arguments for the affirmative offered by a distinguished defender of the compatibility of these two modes of explanation, and I hope to show that his arguments are not only inconclusive, but lead to inescapable contradictions.


DOING, CAUSING AND CAUSING-TO-DO

*Taylor's Two Theses*
Richard Taylor's *Action and Purpose*[13] attempts to drive still deeper the logical wedge inserted by Wittgenstein and Ryle between discourse about human actions and discourse about natural events and processes. Taylor explores the notions of cause, power, action, will, reasons, deliberation and purpose in an effort to show that explaining why a person performs an action is a quite different matter from explaining why a water-pipe bursts or why leaves turn brown in autumn. In this endeavour he adds fuel to the controversy that has been raging in recent years between scientific determinists and the new wave of anti-determinists who hold, not so much that actions are *un*caused, as that, like numbers, possibilities and jokes, they are not the sort of things of which it makes sense either to ascribe or to deny a cause, in any sense of 'cause' that would give comfort to scientific determinism.[14]

Taylor's discussion of the language of action is elegantly lucid, refreshingly non-technical and forcefully stated, although many of his arguments, which were previously formulated by Melden, Peters, Kenny and others, have been challenged by a number of writers in defence of scientific determinism, and it is a bit disappointing that Taylor does not trouble to meet their objections, a fault which I shall try to rectify in the next section of this chapter. The most original aspect of Taylor's approach is his starting-point, although this, as we shall see in the final section, is also the most dubious aspect. Instead of beginning, as Melden, Peters and Kenny did, with the concepts of action, intention and purpose, and exploring the logical differences between these concepts and those of natural science, Taylor begins with the 'metaphysical' concept of causation and tries to show that the original (and he thinks still the correct) concept of cause was that of an animate substance, exercising his power to produce objects or changes in his environment. Taylor argues persuasively that his notion of cause and its cognate notion of power cannot be reduced, à la Hume, to mere invariant succession of events. He then attacks the volitional theory of human action, arguing, along much the same lines as Melden and Kenny, that alleged mental causes of actions, such as volitions, have neither explanatory value nor intrinsic intelligibility. In the remainder of the book he argues persuasively that the appropriate type of explanation of human actions is purposive rather than causal, and that the former is not reducible to the latter.

Taylor's major thesis is that the psychological concepts employed to explain voluntary human actions, concepts like motive, intention, desire and reason, are not causal concepts. The explanations they provide are not predictive in function, since their use presupposes that the agent who performed action A could have refrained from doing A. His arguments, most of which have already been stated by the predecessors mentioned, but which he formulates with special sharpness and verve are: (1) The notion of (voluntary) human action, to which motivational concepts apply, entails that of power or ability, and this notion entails causal indeterminism. 'I can move my finger' . . . entails . . . that whether or not I *do* move my finger is 'up to me' or 'within my power'. (2) Motivational concepts have no predictive value, because they are *ex post facto*. 'Our entire *criterion* for saying what he wanted (or tried or intended or whatnot) to do, is what he in fact did.' (p. 52) (3) If motivational concepts referred either to mental causes or to brain states then the behaviour they are alleged to cause would not be voluntary action; it would not be what the agent does but something that happens to him, like a sneeze or a spasm (p. 73). (4) The relation between motives and actions is logical rather than causal, since motives can be identified only in terms of the actions they motivate.[15]

These four arguments which, for the sake of brevity of reference, I shall dub (1) the 'up to me', (2) the *ex post facto*, (3) the 'uncontrollable reflex' and (4) the 'logical connection' arguments, have a strong intrinsic plausibility because, I believe, they are on the right track, but as Taylor states them, they are inconclusive. The *ex post facto* argument is simply a corollary of the logical connection argument; the uncontrollable reflex argument (that if my action is caused then it is not an action but something that happens to me like a sneeze) begs the question, since the determinist can and does reply that sneezes are one kind of happening and voluntary actions are another; the 'up to me' argument, that voluntary action entails the power to do or to refrain, is obscure, because Taylor insists that his notion of power is unanalysable, and if so, we have no criterion for determining when an agent has or fails to have such power; finally, the fourth argument, that there is a logical bond between motivating state and action is inconclusive because the nature of this bond is not spelled out, nor is it proved that such a bond exists. While the logical connection argument, drawn from Wittgenstein and Melden, seems to me the most promising, it has been powerfully attacked in recent literature, and, if it is to be made convincing, the objections raised by determinists should be met and the nature of the logical bond should be made clear. In the part that follows, I shall try to do just this – to defend Taylor's logical connection argument against Davidson, Goldberg, Gean and others, and to make more clear just what the logical connection is, from which it will follow that Taylor is right to maintain that reasons, intentions, etc. are not causes of actions. In the last section of this chapter I shall criticise what I believe to be unnecessary concessions to determinism made by Taylor, to the effect that actions may be caused by events *other than* motivating states; concessions which seem to me to render his entire theory of action incoherent. The reason for these self-defeating concessions on Taylor's part lies, I think, in his failure to distinguish three quite different things, namely, doing, causing and causing to do. If I succeed in establishing these two theses, (1) the pro-Taylor thesis that voluntary actions are not caused by motivating states and (2) my own anti-Taylor thesis that voluntary actions are not caused by anything *other than* motivating states, then it will follow that voluntary actions are not caused at all, a conclusion whose importance I need not spell out.

### In Defence of Taylor's First Thesis

The Melden–Kenny–Taylor thesis, that actions are not caused by reasons, intentions, motives, decisions or purposes, as supported by the logical connection argument, has been attacked by many determinists, most notably by Davidson, Kim, and Brandt, Hempel, Goldberg, Berofsky, Gean, Margolis, Kaplan, and A. C. Macintyre.[16] Davidson and Goldberg question whether there is in fact a logical rather than a causal connection between motive and act and argue that, even if there were, it would not be of the type that excludes a causal relation. Davidson argues that the relation between a reason or motive and an act is like that between a physical disposition such as brittleness of glass and an event such as the glass breaking under an impact. The brittleness, together with a trigger event, say the impact of a stone, causally explains the shattering of glass, and similarly, a motivating state together with some stimulus event causally explains an action. Much could be said about the defects of this analogy between psychological states and physical dispositions, but space does not allow an exploration of that point here. I want only to make the general comment that Davidson's notion of causal explanation is a tenuous bridge straddling a metaphysical chasm between two totally different kinds of explanation which, for various historical and psychological reasons, most of them consisting in philosophical mistakes, have been confused by every determinist. The two kinds of explanations generally confused are: explaining what caused event E to occur, and explaining what caused agent X to perform action A. I shall postpone the exploration of this chasm until later, pausing only to remark that Richard Taylor, disdaining Davidson's unstable bridge, tries bravely to leap across the chasm but doesn't quite make it to the other side.

Does a logical bond between motive and act exclude a causal one? Davidson, in 'Actions, Reasons and Causes' daringly says no. He considers it a false cliché to insist that causes must be logically independent of their effects, and he denies, or appears to deny, that a causal relation is always an empirical one. With eye-raising bravado, he declares:

> In any case there is something very odd in the idea that causal relations are empirical rather than logical. What can this mean? Surely not that any true causal statement is empirical. For suppose A caused B to be true. Then the cause of B=A; so substituting, we have 'The cause of B caused B' which is analytic.[17]

Davidson here interprets the claim that causal relations are empirical as equivalent to the obviously absurd claim that, to use his own words, 'any true causal statement is empirical', where, by 'causal statement' he obviously means any statement involving the word 'cause'. But few who assert the first would assert the second, and no one would regard them as equivalent. The anti-determinist's point is not that *no* statement involving the word 'cause' is analytic (what about 'A cause is a cause'?), but only that no successful attempt at a *causal explanation*, i.e. no statement that significantly asserts a causal relation to hold between two events is analytic. Surely Davidson would not want to hold that his sentence, 'The cause of B caused B' provides a *causal explanation* of B? It seems as odd to me that Davidson should wonder why other people assert that causal relations are empirical as it seems odd to him that they do assert this.

Bruce Goldberg, in an article in *Analysis*,[18] follows Davidson's lead in attacking the logical connection argument, and, trying to cross the same untenable bridge between motives and causes, falls gallantly with Davidson into the metaphysical chasm.

Goldberg argues that the apparent force of the logical connection argument (i.e. the argument that motives cannot be causes because causes are contingently linked to their effects while motives are logically bound to the actions they motivate) rests on a confusion between events themselves and the particular *descriptions* under which we refer to them. If C is the cause of E, C can always be described in terms of E or E in terms of C, without thereby making one a logical function of the other. Thus, as Davidson had already pointed out, we can answer the question 'What happened to Jones?' by saying 'He was burned', thus redescribing the effect, Jones' injury, in terms of the cause, the event of his contact with intense heat. 'The *truth* of a causal statement', says Davidson, very sensibly, 'depends on *what* events are described; its status as analytic or synthetic depends on *how* the events are described.'[19] This is of course perfectly true, but it completely misses the point of the Melden–Taylor logical connection argument. For the crucial point about motives is that they are not only *sometimes* described in terms of the actions they are alleged to cause, but that this is the *only* way they can *possibly* be described and identified.

Now Goldberg, in his gloss on Davidson, notices the difference between a description of C *necessarily* involving reference to E and its only *happening* to involve E, but he argues that even such necessary involvement does not preclude causality, since from the fact that the *description* of the motive necessarily involves reference to the action 'It does not follow that the *occurrence* [of the motive, R.A.] entails the *occurrence* of the action. If I want to go to the theater, does it follow that I go to the theater? There are at least some occasions when we don't do what we want to do.'

Goldberg's argument sounds eminently plausible, but only because he assumes, like most determinists, and even many anti-determinists who are muddled on this issue, that the relation between motive and action, if it is to be a logical bond, must be the relation of unrestricted entailment i.e. that a motive for doing action A must entail that the agent actually does A. And of course, such a position is plain silly. But from the silliness of *this* conception of the logical bond between motive and act, it does not follow that there is no logical bond at all. The true bond, it seems to me, is that of contextually limited entailment between motive and act. I shall not develop the point fully here,[20] but briefly, it goes like this: Assume that Jones wants, intends, desires, or in some sense has a motive to open the window. What does this entail about what he will do? Well, it entails that he will open the window, but it does not entail this *tout court*. It entails that he will open the window *provided* that no reason arises for his not doing so (e.g. a hurricane is not blowing outside) and provided nothing prevents him (e.g. he is not paralysed and the window isn't stuck). The provisos here constitute the contextual limitation I spoke of on the entailment between motive and act. To say 'I want to open the window, nothing prevents me and I have no reason or motive not to, not even the motive of laziness, but still I won't open the window' is senseless. What on earth could I mean by 'want'? In this contextually limited way, a motive is indeed logically connected to an action, and not just through the way that it happens to be described, and not just to the concept of the action, but to its actual performance.

I turn now to an article by W. D. Gean entitled 'Reasons and Causes'[21] in which Gean tries to cross the Davidson bridge with equally disastrous effect. Gean too wants to show that reasons and motives can be causes. Like Davidson, he concentrates on the word 'reason' rather than motive words like 'want', 'intend', 'decide', etc. This move of Davidson and Gean produces a particularly creaky coupling for their bridge. There is at least some specious plausibility in taking motivating states like wanting and intending to be causes of actions, but to take reasons as causes requires unusual insensitivity to the nuances of the English language. For reasons are things that need not even exist, and how can something *cause* something else if it doesn't exist? That this room is on fire may be my reason for rushing out of it, even if the room is not on fire. But if not, how can the non-existent fact of the room being on fire cause me to rush out? Gean and Davidson might reply that both the reason and cause of my rushing out is, not the *fact* of the room being on fire, but my belief that it is on fire. But this is simply an additional linguistic error. Beliefs count as reasons only in very special cases. If I believe I am Napoleon, that is a good reason for me to consult a psychiatrist. For here, the fact which constitutes a reason for my action is the fact that I believe something. But in the earlier example of my rushing out of the room, it was not the fact that I believed something that constituted, for me, a reason to rush out; rather it was the *content* of my belief, namely, the fact that the room is on fire, that was my reason for rushing out. To put it simply, I run away from real or imaginary fires, not from my beliefs, except in the special cases where my beliefs themselves are objects of dread, such as the belief that I am Napoleon.

Before leaving all this wreckage due to Davidson's bridge and turning to observe Taylor's fatal jump, I would like to consider one very important further point made by Gean, a point that will lead me into my criticism of Richard Taylor's second thesis in the next section.

Gean's additional argument that reasons are also causes is based on an appeal to ordinary discourse. It is, he points out, a noteworthy fact that statements explaining action in terms of reasons are translatable into statements explaining them in terms of causes.[22] For example, the explanation, 'His reason for leaving the party early was that he had a later appointment' could be restated as 'Having a later appointment caused him to leave the party early'. Similarly, 'The reason for the ambassador's protest was the President's remarks' can be translated without loss into 'The President's remarks caused the ambassador to protest'.[23]

Now this argument would be convincing if we were to assume, as Gean does, that the difference between A causing B and A causing B *to do* C is so insignificant as to be safely ignored. But the difference between causing and causing to do happens to be a deceptive looking fissure that, on further exploration, widens into a metaphysical gulf precisely as vast as that between reasons and causes. To see this, we need only look for the *dis*analogies between reason language and causal language, after having granted Gean the analogy on which he rests his case. With what *other* types of locutions does 'causing to do' (as distinguished from merely causing) freely mingle? Does not 'causing to do' belong to a family of locutions such as 'bribing', 'inciting', 'persuading', 'convincing', 'coercing', and do not all these locutions indicate different ways of doing the same general thing, namely providing an agent with a reason for performing a certain action? Now contrast this behaviour of 'causing to do' with the simpler expression, just plain 'causing', as when we say that heat caused an explosion, or the failure of the brake caused the accident. Could we replace the sentence, 'The sudden heat caused the explosion' with any substitute of the form 'The sudden heat persuaded, incited, bribed or coerced the explosion'? Clearly, plain causing goes with producing, making, bringing about, and other such locutions, while 'causing to do' belongs to quite a different family, namely, the reason-offering family.

## Critique of Taylor's Second Thesis

After having defended Taylor's first and, I think, true thesis, that motives are not causes, I turn now to his second and, I think, false thesis, that actions may have causes *other* than motives. But here we must distinguish between three different contentions, the first of which is rightly rejected by Taylor, while the second and third are wrongly defended by him:

1. Actions are physical events caused by antecedent physical events.
2. Actions are caused or brought about by persons.
3. The agents who perform actions may be, and perhaps are always, caused to perform them.[24]

Contention 1 above has been adequately criticised by Melden, Richard Taylor and Charles Taylor.[25] The argument of Melden and Richard Taylor is that, if actions were explainable as necessary results of antecedent events other than the agent's intentions or purposes, then the agent would have to perform them whether he wanted to or not; thus all actions would turn out to be non-voluntary. The agent would be a 'helpless victim' of the forces compelling him to act, as he clearly is in the case of a muscular spasm or a sneeze. Charles Taylor's argument is more theoretical and, I think, more compelling: If all actions could be explained by antecedent physical events, then there would be no need for psychological explanation in terms of intentions, motives, reasons, etc. Thus all genuinely psychological concepts would be empirically vacuous. He does not deny the possibility that behavioural sciences of the future may come up with adequate causal explanations of all human actions in terms of conditioning processes and neural events, but merely points out that the weight of the available empirical evidence is overwhelmingly to the contrary, so that the thesis of naturalistic determinism is a faith in defiance of the known facts.

Contention 2 is an interesting ploy proposed by Richard Taylor, who disinters the ancient conception of a person as a 'first cause' of his actions. Now there would be no strong objection to this way of putting things (which has at least the merit of reminding us that actions are not caused by antecedent events) were it not for its misleading suggestion (contrary to the main thesis of Taylor's book) that actions are explainable in the same *sort* of way as physical events. It appeals most strongly to those who are wedded to the *a priori* principle that everything has some kind of cause and who reason that, if an action is not caused by an event or process, then it must be caused by an agent. But this account is a misleading attempt to have the best of two incompatible worlds. For what is really gained in the way of understanding by saying that a person *causes* his actions rather than just saying that he *performs* them or *does* them? Are we not forcing language to fit a theory of causality? Ordinarily, when we attribute causal agency to a person, we refer to some event that he brought about *by means* of his actions, as when we say 'Smith caused the accident'. Smith's action, in such case, consists precisely in his *causing of the accident*, so that, if we were to say that he caused his *action*, we would be asserting that he was the cause of causing the accident, thus launching into an infinite regress.

The trouble with Taylor's account of agency is that he is not clear enough on just what he regards the agent as the cause *of*. The second term of his causal relation vacillates between (a) the action, (b) the bodily motion involved in the action, and (c) the event or state of affairs brought about by means of the action.[26] But these are very different matters. It is one thing to assert that an agent causes his own action, quite another to assert that he causes the bodily movement in which his action consists, and still another to say that he causes the state of affairs resulting from his action. The first two claims are, I think, incoherent, while only the third makes clear sense. For consider:

(a) The claim that a person causes his action; what more does it say than that he simply does it? If it says anything more, it suggests that the agent makes his action happen, that he brings it about. But can an action be made to happen or be brought about? I can make it happen that a light goes on by raising my hand and pressing a switch, but can I 'make it happen' that I raise my hand? If so, how? Where we speak of making things happen we take responsibility for being able to describe the means or manner by which we get them done. Yet, as Taylor himself observes, we cannot describe how we perform what he calls 'simple acts'. The question 'How?' makes no sense. We just do them. But if so, then it is very misleading to insist that we cause them. Moreover, if we were really to consider an agent as the cause of his acts, we would, as Taylor himself argues when he criticises the 'volitional theory of action' (yet somehow forgets when he pushes his own agent-as-cause theory), commit ourselves to the assumption that the agent and his act are separately identifiable entities. Yet a moment's reflection is enough to see that this violates the logical grammar (shall we say 'ontology'?) of all inter-translatable natural languages. We cannot *fully* identify a particular action without identifying the person who performed it. My action of raising my hand is not the same as your action of raising your (nor even my) hand.

(b) Can the agent be the cause of the bodily movement involved in or constituting his action? If I raise my hand, am I the cause, not of raising my hand, but of the event of my hand rising? Taylor, following Wittgenstein, maintains that there is nothing left if we subtract my hand going up from raising my hand. But then, if it is senseless to say that I cause my raising my hand, it must be just as senseless to say that I cause my hand to rise. For these are not different events, but the same event under different descriptions. Moreover, if I am said to cause or bring about my hand's going up, as we ordinarily use this locution, it would imply that I do something simpler, M, which results in the movement of my hand. If my right hand were paralysed, I might grasp it with my left and force it to go up, in which case I would indeed have caused my right hand to go up, and I could easily explain how I brought this about. But in the case of a 'simple act', i.e. an act that is not analysable into component acts, no such explanation is possible. Thus, if my act is a simple one, it makes no sense to say that I cause it, while if it is complex, then we can distinguish the simple act M, which I just do, from the later event or state of affairs, E, which I bring about by means of M. In such case, I can indeed be said to have caused E, but it can as well be said that *my action M* was the cause of E. Thus Taylor is quite mistaken in thinking that the notion of a substantial agent as cause of his bodily movements is essential to action discourse, for any reference to the agent as cause of E can be replaced by reference to his doing M as the cause of E, and it is once again obvious that doing is not the same sort of thing as causing.

(c) What, finally, of the agent as the cause of the state of affairs E brought about by means of his simple act M, or (more often) by a series of simple acts $M_n$ into which the gross notion of an action such as robbing a bank is usually analysable?[27]

This possibility has already been sufficiently explored in passing, and we have found it to be the only intelligible one of the three alternatives between which Taylor vacillates. It is, then, perfectly sound to say that I am the cause of whatever I accomplish or bring about. But it is just as sound to say that my actions $M_n$ are the cause, so that there is really no need to revive the archaic notion of a substantial 'first cause'.

Contention 3: Having considered and found incoherent the contentions 1 (that actions are physical events caused by antecedent physical events) and 2 (that actions are caused by agents) let us turn to contention 3, the interesting claim made by Taylor that an agent may be caused by some event to perform an action and thus, in Taylor's language, may be caused to cause an action. It is primarily on this ground that Taylor argues that the differences he explores between action discourse and discourse about natural events do not disprove determinism, since the fact that an agent is a first cause of action does not preclude that he may be caused to act as he does, thus forming part of a deterministic chain. This position seems to me hopelessly inconsistent.

At various points in his book, Taylor offers four examples of situations compatible both with his analysis of action language and with scientific determinism. It will be useful to examine each of these examples separately:

(a) The case where an agent is moved by unconscious psychic forces, as when one asks a guest to leave, giving the reason that he is spoiling the party, but really motivated by a deep resentment, formed in early childhood, toward some relative whom the guest resembles.[28]

(b) The case where an agent is caused to perform an action (such as moving his foot) by post-hypnotic suggestion.[29]

(c) Being caused by some frightening stimulus to act in an excessive or irrational way, as when one grasps one's seat tightly on a ski lift when it suddenly accelerates.[30]

(d) Being coerced into acting contrary to one's normal desires as when one is 'driven to his action by threats'.[31]

(a) Are unconscious desires, phobias, etc. natural causes, or are they more like reasons and purposes which the agent happens to conceal (more or less successfully) from himself and from others? A. C. Macintyre has argued persuasively for the latter interpretation in his book *The Unconscious*. If he is correct, then our case (a) is not a genuine case of causality *along with* action done for a reason, but only an especially complicated case of the latter. On the other hand, if Macintyre is wrong and the orthodox Freudian account of the unconscious in terms of 'psychodynamic forces' is literally true, then the agent's explanation of his action as done for a reason (to prevent the guest from spoiling the party) is either insincere or self-deceptive. In fact, he was, in Taylor's own language, 'a helpless victim' of forces beyond his control. Philosophers and psychoanalysts are still divided as to which of these two interpretations is correct, but only Richard Taylor seems willing to accept *both*. Moreover, on the second interpretation, we can then ask, what is it that the psychodynamic forces of the agent's unconscious can be said to cause; do they cause the agent's bodily movements, or do they cause his actions? If the former, then, on Taylor's own analysis, the agent's movements are not actions but happenings, like sneezes and spasms. If the latter, then the actions can be causally explained without reference to the agent's purposes and intentions, which contradicts Taylor's major thesis that non-causal intentions and purposes are essential to the explanation of actions.

(b) Actions due to post-hypnotic suggestions raise a similar problem of dual interpretation. Some experts on hypnosis claim that we cannot be made to do by hypnosis anything that we really do not want to do. If they are right, then hypnotic suggestion does not cause us to act, but only provides us with further inducements or reasons (such as the encouragement of a father-figure) for acting as suggested. If they are wrong, then hypnotic acts are in fact determined by psychic forces but, in that case, they occur independently of our intentions and outside of our control and thus, on Taylor's own account, they are not actions at all. The apparent plausibility of Taylor's example of hypnosis, like his example of unconsciously motivated behaviour, is due to the ease with which he and we shift inadvertently between the causal and the purposive interpretations of abnormal behaviour.

(c) Grasping one's seat on a ski lift because of a frightening sudden acceleration is a more challenging case. Taylor argues persuasively that such a response is genuinely the agent's action rather than a mere happening, yet the stimulus appears to be a cause that triggers the response as a lighted fuse triggers an explosion. But here again, the plausibility of the example is due to a concealed ambiguity in the description. If I am challenged not to grasp my seat, or perhaps offered a desirable reward for refraining, and I do refrain, then clearly the action is at least semi-voluntary and it is not a *necessary* consequence of the frightening stimulus. If, on the other hand, no inducement can succeed in inhibiting my fear response, then, although perhaps it is too complex and skilful a response to classify it as a reflex, it is at least very much like a reflex in that it is not within my control and thus not *my* action in the agency sense of 'my', thus not an action at all according to Taylor's analysis of 'action'. We often call such responses 'involuntary actions'. It is not to me a matter of great concern whether we call them actions or just responses.

(d) The case of coerced action is the most interesting. Can coercion such as threat of bodily or financial injury *literally* be considered the cause of an action? Or is it rather a strong excusing or justifying *reason* for doing what one is commanded to do? I believe the latter account to be correct, for three reasons: (i) Coercion-action is always mediated by the agent's beliefs and evaluations; whether or not I bow to a threat depends on my understanding the threat and believing that it will be carried out and also on my valuing my life or my fortune more than what I will lose by knuckling under. (ii) There are not now, and there is no ground for believing there ever will be, known laws that link specific coercions with specific actions. Even in the most extreme cases of bodily torture or threat to destroy the victim's family, sufficient counter-examples have already been recorded in history against the cliché that such threats are irresistible.[32] (iii) What kinds of things could count as coercive 'causes'? Are they mere physical stimuli such as the shape of a gun or a thunderous shout? Clearly not so, since we must *interpret* these events as threatening before we respond to them as such. If I believe that the gun pointed at me is only a toy, I will not be coerced to open the safe even if the gun really is loaded. But then, if coercions are what we believe to be the case, rather than what in fact is the case, either they are the very 'mental occurrences' which Taylor for very sound reasons repudiates as a useless and inconsistent hypothesis, or they are not occurrences at all but simply good or bad *reasons* for the actions they explain.

I believe this last account to be the true one, but in any case it seems clear that coercion is not causation, except in the same metaphorical sense in which we might speak of ethical causality, as when we say: 'My sense of duty caused me to do it; I had no choice.' And surely Taylor would not be tempted to take this *façon de parler* at face value.

In general if, as Taylor himself contends, actions are not caused by antecedent events, but only by agents, then what can be his meaning in claiming that an antecedent event can cause an agent to perform an action? Is the entity, agent-to-perform-the-action (or, in better grammar, the -agent's-performance-of-the-action) the second term of a causal relation of which the first term is an antecedent event, such as the threat of death? Presumably Taylor is claiming just this, but the immediate difficulty faced by such a position is that there is none but a superficial grammatical difference between an action and the agent's performance of it; the action just *is* the agent's performance. Flicking a light switch is not an individual action but a type of action until it is individuated with respect to place, time and agency. Thus if an antecedent event of any kind, mental or physical, purposive or mechanical, could cause an agent's-performance-of-an-action, then it could be said to cause the action, *tout court*. But this is inconsistent with Taylor's contention that actions are caused only by agents. Now we have already seen that it is either misleadingly vacuous or downright false to say that agents or their intentions are the causes of actions. If these alternatives are exhaustive, as it seems to me they are, then it clearly follows that actions are not caused by anything.

# 4 Motivation

'Love is not a feeling. Love is put to the test, pain not. One does not say: "That was not true pain, or it would not have gone off so quickly" ' – Wittgenstein, *Zettel*

If psychological description and explanation are rational, rather than causal, terminating in reasons and avowals, rather than in initial conditions and laws, then what is the relation between reasons for actions and the family of motivational concepts whose central members are 'want', 'desire', and 'emotion'? I shall argue that motivational concepts, which are crucial to psychological explanation, are not themselves reasons for actions, but that their meanings essentially involve reasons; and then I shall try to sketch out the remaining components of their meanings so as to explain why such concepts seem to, yet in reality do not, refer either to introspectable private mental states, or to observable physiological states, nor even to Rylean dispositions, although they do involve physical states and behavioural dispositions in an interestingly complex and heretofore misunderstood way.

Let us begin at the periphery, and work our way toward the centre. Before dealing directly with the 'internal states' of wanting, desiring and emotion, let us first consider some derivative uses of 'want', etc. in explaining human actions, namely, first-person locutions of the form, 'Because I want to A', where the values of the variable 'A' are actions.

## REASONS AND REASON TERMINATORS

My claim, in support of Peters, Dray and Melden, that psychological explanation is non-causal and that it is logically bound up with normative judgment or justification, may seem least plausible when one considers 'explanations' of the form, 'Because I wanted to do it' (or liked to, had a desire to, etc.). Wanting, liking and enjoying are not reasons as I have defined 'reason'; they are not statements that one can appeal to in supporting, recommending or justifying actions. On the contrary, they are thought to motivate action in defiance of moral or even self-serving normative judgment. Thus they play no role in justification yet they do seem to perform some kind of explanatory function. Since they are not rationally explanatory, are they then causally explanatory? I think not. They are neither reasons nor causes but they are, I think, logically linked to reasons.

Prior to this century, when psychology was still a branch of speculative philosophy, psychologists and philosophers argued endlessly as to whether all actions are motivated by pleasure, desire or need. Freud was sufficiently steeped in this kind of causal psychology to search for 'unconscious' desires, needs and pleasures when no such 'motives' were obvious either to the agent or to the close observer. Ryle attempted to put this way of thinking to rest once and for all by arguing that the concepts of pleasure, want, enjoyment and the like are not names of internal events and therefore not the causal springs of action. They are, for Ryle, dispositional concepts that licence predictions about a person's behaviour. To say that one enjoys fishing, or that he wants very much to fish is, for Ryle, to predict that he will frequently go to some trouble to fish, that he will fish with energy and concentration, and that he will be restless and distracted when prevented from fishing.

Kurt Baier, in *The Moral Point of View*, classifies likes, wants, desires and pleasures as 'self-regarding reasons' for action, on the ground that saying 'Because I like to' (or want to, etc.) is a possible reply to the question, 'Why are you doing that?'[1] I think that Baier is mistaken. As Melden has observed, we often respond to the question 'Why did you do that?' by saying, 'No reason. I just wanted to' (or like to). The appropriateness of the introductory phrase, 'No reason' cannot be disregarded. After all, I do not *need* a reason for doing what I like to do or want to do. If anything, I need strong reasons to refrain from such activities. But if wants, desires, likes, etc. are neither causes nor reasons, then what is the explanatory role of the locutions, 'Because I want to', 'Because I like to', etc.?

Suppose that, at a dramatic moment in a bridge game, Mr Jones's foot is observed to come into violent contact with Mrs Jones's shin. We ask Mr Jones, 'Why on earth did you kick your wife?' and he replies, 'Because she trumped my ace'. He thus explains his action by citing a reason which, in his system of values, justifies it: If Mr Jones frequently behaves in this way there seems little doubt that he has adequately explained himself; the reason he gave is, in fact, the motive for his action. But we need not consider it a good reason.

Now let us suppose that instead of giving us a reason, Mr Jones replies: 'No reason. I just wanted to (or like to) kick her.' What would be the point of this reply, and what explanatory value would it have?

On the causal theory of psychological explanation, Mr Jones would have explained his action by identifying the psychic stimulus to which his action was a necessary response. But if this were so, then we would be obliged to admit that Mr Jones could not have refrained from kicking his wife, since he was the helpless victim of an irresistible psychic force, just as much as if he had said: 'I didn't kick her. It just happened that my foot twitched violently.' Yet clearly, this is wrong. The right attitude to take toward Mr Jones's reply is to condemn him as a vicious sadist.

Would it then be correct to say with Ryle that Mr Jones has given us a law-like description of his characteristic behaviour and thereby provided us with a licence to predict that, under similar conditions, he will kick his wife again, and that he will do so with enthusiasm and with undivided attention? I think not, for two reasons. First, while we might infer all this information from Mr Jones's reply, he did not actually *tell* us all this. All he said was 'Because I wanted to'. Secondly, the Rylean expansion, like the causal interpretation, fails to reveal why Mr Jones's reply is morally objectionable. If Mr Jones has merely given us a true explanation of his conduct, then why do we feel that Mr Jones, in replying as he did, has added insult to injury? The trouble with the Rylean interpretation is that it parallels the causal one, and merely substitutes a physical stimulus for a psychic stimulus, while transferring the psychic aspect to the law-like relation between stimulus and response. Like the paramechanical view that he opposes, Ryle's view too leaves no place for moral responsibility, since the action remains a necessary effect of causal antecedents.[2]

Baier's view, that 'Because I wanted to' states a selfish reason for the action, does a bit more justice to the ethical significance of Mr Jones's reply, but it is still not satisfactory. For it fails to explain why the reply is so *remarkably* offensive. Baier's interpretation would place 'Because I wanted to' on the same ethical level as 'Because she trumped my ace', in classifying both responses as bad reasons. But the reasons of fanatical bridge players, bad as they are, are surely less repugnant than the defiance of a sadist. 'Because I wanted to' is objectionable, not only because it fails to offer a good reason for Mr Jones's act, but more than that, because it fails to offer *any* reason, and it implies that no reason need be given. Mr Jones was not pleading his case for acquittal. He was denying the jurisdiction of the court.

Saying that one likes, enjoys, wants or desires to do something gives neither a cause nor a reason for the deed, but it is intimately related to reasons. Nowell-Smith and A. I. Melden have suggested that these locutions deny the need for reasons. Their function is not to explain any action, but to indicate that no further explanation is in order because the process of rational deliberation (giving B as a reason for A, C as a reason for B, etc.) terminates at this point.[3] We might call this the limiting or 'null' case of rational explanation. 'I just wanted to' informs us that it is not our business to demand reasons, and it is sometimes the appropriate response to make. In the absence of reasons against, a man's activities are his private affair.

'Because I want to' (or like to, desire to, etc.) may then be said to function as *reason-terminating* locutions. They indicate, in various ways, that there is no point to further discussion, and they are appropriate responses when there really is no point; otherwise they are extremely offensive. In a rather similar way, 'Do as you like' and 'Do whatever you want' indicate that the speaker has no reasons to offer for or against any course of action favoured by the agent. 'Because I want to' is the agent's way of terminating rational deliberation. 'Do as you want' is the spectator's way.

REASON TERMINATORS AND EXPLANATION

But reason-terminating locutions are not all alike. An adequate account of them must do justice to two features that have so far been left out of consideration: (1) The fact that some of these expressions have more explanatory power and informative value than others and (2) the striking difference of tone between say, 'Because I like to do it' and 'Because I had an overwhelming desire to do it'.

1. I began this discussion with Ryle's dispositional analysis of wanting, liking, enjoyment and the like, and I criticised it for not accounting for the reason-terminating function of these concepts. But I should like now to make use of Ryle's insights by qualifying what I have said so far. I have considered only the common features of reason-terminating locutions. But there are conspicuous differences. Some are more informative and therefore more satisfactory explanations than others. Suppose that you and I are sitting in my living-room. Suddenly I jump up and hurl my chair through the nearest window pane. You exclaim 'Why on earth did you do that?' Now suppose I reply, 'Because I wanted to'. You would be perfectly entitled to protest, 'That's no explanation!' 'Because I wanted to' is just about the most uninformative and unsatisfactory reply I could make to your request for an explanation. It tells you nothing except that what I did is none of your business. (It does not even inform you that my action was intentional, since you already assume this when you demand a purposive explanation.)

Now suppose that I say, instead, 'Because I had an intense desire (or need or craving) to do it'. You would then learn something about me, to wit, that I am a bit mad; something is going on inside me that may explode on other occasions besides this one.

If my reply were 'Because I like to throw chairs through windows' or 'Because I enjoy doing this', you would also come to understand that I am mad, and more than just a bit. For I would be informing you that, as Ryle would put it, this is the sort of impractical conduct I am likely to engage in whenever circumstances permit. Thus 'Because I like to' and 'Because I have a desire to' do more than terminate rational discussion. They also relate the action in question to one's

general pattern of behaviour and in this respect they have explanatory
value. 'Explanation' in the widest sense means showing how something unexpected might, with more information, have been expected.
Reason-terminating locutions can play an explanatory role, although
they provide neither causes nor reasons for action, by revealing features
of one's character that make the action more predictable. Ryle's dispositional account of wanting, liking and enjoyment was therefore on
the right track, although it did not go far enough because it ignored
their reason-terminating role, and also because 'I like', 'I desire', etc.
do not *assert* this general information about one's character, but rather,
in various ways which I shall presently consider, they suggest or
symptomatise such information.

2. There is a conspicuous difference in tone between the expressions
'Because I had an intense desire (or craving) to do it', and 'Because I
like to do it (or enjoy doing it)'. The first type of locution has a note
of desperate urgency, it sounds grim and pathetic, while the second
type sounds gay, frivolous and complacent. When both types are considered as reason terminators symptomatic of the speaker's character
and personality, this difference in tone is easily explained. Such locutions terminate rational discussion *for various motives*, and, as we have
seen, motives (as distinct from possible reasons) are rooted in character.
These locutions do not *state* one's motive for an act, but they are
motivated by and thus symptomatic of certain attitudes. Intense desire,
need and want are alleged when one feels guilty about his action (hence
the pathos), while liking, enjoyment and pleasure are alleged when one
feels innocent, lighthearted or defiant. 'Because I had an intense desire
(need, or craving) to do it' suggests to us that the speaker knows there
are strong reasons, either moral or practical, against his action, but he
was unable to control himself, not in the way he cannot control the
weather, but in the way that one cannot help scratching an itch or
drinking heavily. We all have our characteristic moments of irrationality. Provided that they are not too frequent and not too harmful to
others, we hope to be forgiven for them. 'Because I wanted (needed or
desired) passionately to do it' terminates rational argument in something like the way a defendant terminates a trial, by pleading guilty
and throwing himself on the mercy of the court. Hence their tone of
desperate pleading.

'Because I like to do it' (or enjoy doing it) terminates rational discussion for a different kind of motive, and symptomatises a different
aspect of the speaker's character. This response suggests, as we have seen,
that the speaker sees no good reason against his action, and it attenuates
our surprise by indicating that the action is characteristic of the agent.
It is a type of action he tends to perform without needing any reasons,
although, of course, he may also do it for a reason. A business man
may play golf because he likes to and also because he meets his clients

on the golf course. 'I like' and 'I enjoy' inform us about the agent's values. Unlike 'Because I had an intense desire (or need or craving) to do it', which admits that what the agent did was bad or wrong, 'Because I like (or enjoy or get pleasure from) it' implies that what the speaker has done is, in his view, generally worth doing and so needs no special justifying reasons. The things we like, enjoy or find pleasant are just those things that provide us with prudential reasons for doing anything else.

REASONS, DESIRES AND FEELINGS

*The role of reasons in purposive explanation*
We explain voluntary actions in two ways: (1) By indicating that the action is one that the agent could be expected to perform under the circumstances (e.g. 'Because I (he) enjoy(s) doing it', 'Because it is my (his) habit to do so', 'Because it was my (his) turn', 'Because Jones asked me (him) to do it', etc.). (2) By assigning to the agent a purpose, or need, or desire and/or rule that explains his action as (for him) a necessary means to a goal G, and in this way shows that the action could have been expected as well as 'holding his conduct up for assessment', as right or wrong, wise or foolish, excusable or culpable.[4]

The motivating purpose, desire and/or reason is logically linked to the specific goal, which is to say that the goal-state G would not *be* a goal for the agent, were he not, on his own view at least, rationally directed toward achieving it. The performance of the action A thus explained as, from the agent's point of view, the necessary means to achieving G, although contingently related to G itself, is entailed by the premisses constituting the *explanans* [namely, that the agent wants, needs or desires G (minor premiss) and that (from his standpoint) A is necessary to achieve G], within the contextual limitations, or *ceteris paribus* conditions indicated in the previous chapter. In the light of this entailment relation, it might appear that a psychological explanation, as I have schematised it, suffers from the vacuity of Molière's 'dormative virtue' pseudo-explanation. But what saves it from such analytic vacuity is the *ceteris paribus* element, for the claim that these conditions hold is a contingent claim.[5]

1. The first mode of explanation, I have argued, is not a reason-giving, but a reason-terminating response to the question, 'Why did X do A?', an explanation, so to speak, of why no reason-giving explanation is in order, insofar as the agent's action is what was to be expected under the circumstances, or insofar as the action, contrary to first appearances, was not rule-violating and thus not in need of justification or excuse.

2. Means–end Purposive Explanation. The most common form of

purposive explanation of action is: 'X did A in order to get G' (or, as we shall later see, 'In doing A, X was accomplishing G'). Clearly, this formula is enthymematic. It takes tacitly for granted that (a) X wanted or desired G and (b) that X believed that A was the most convenient, appropriate or, in some sense necessary means to achieve G.

We often say, X's reason for doing A was to get G. Is the goal of an action, then, in itself the *reason* for the action? Surely not, if the goal object or state is described independently of the agent's rules and values. Objects and states, no matter how desirable, are not *reasons* which, as we have already noted, are abstract, conceptual entities, like corporations, numbers and laws. It has already been suggested that reasons are argument-premises, thus propositions and rules appealed to in support of a conclusion. But if so, then what do they have to do with goals, which are states, events and objects? (If it be argued, as A. Kenny does, that a goal is not a desired *object*, but only the state of achieving and possessing an object, consider that an artist, creating a sculpture, painting, composition or poem, aims at bringing into existence an art object, not his own state of satisfaction. Were he to aim at the latter, he need only swallow a tranquilliser.[6])

I suggest that a reason is (a) a logical link between an action and its goal, in the form of a rule, '*Ceteris paribus*, doing A is necessary to get G', or (b) a logical link between rule and action, by indicating the goal. In a practical syllogism, the full argument for the performance of A would be: 'I (you, he) want G, doing A is necessary to get G, therefore it is necessary (i.e. right, appropriate, advisable, etc.) that I (you, he) do A.' Either the major premiss (the rule) or the minor premiss (indication of the goal aimed at) can be considered the reason(s) for doing A, depending on what we take for granted, in contrast with what we want to know to satisfy us as an explanation.

For example, if we ask 'Why did Jones open the window?' because we want to know what Jones was trying to achieve, the reason (i.e. missing link in the explanation) might be, 'To air out the room'. For in such case, the rule at work, 'Opening a window is the way to air out a room', can be taken for granted. But suppose the event occurs in London during the Second World War and the room is illuminated, so that the appropriate rule here is 'To air out a room, it is necessary to install a blackout curtain, *not* to open a window'. In such a context, we would want to know what, if any countervailing rule Jones was acting on (was he obeying the orders of a treacherous superior officer, was he himself acting for the enemy?) or whether Jones was simply ignorant of the prevailing rule. It would not be an adequate explanation to say, simply, 'He opened the window to air out the room'. One does not air out a room by getting the roof blown off by a bomb.

If we see Jones sawing and nailing pieces of wood and we ask, 'Why are you doing that?' we usually want to know what result he is trying to achieve. Often, in such cases, we ask '*What* are you doing?' where the description we want classifies the simple actions we observe under a complex activity that includes the goal, e.g. 'I am making a cabinet'. Only if Jones appears to us to be following the wrong procedure, either in pursuing *this* goal when he ought to be, say, mowing the lawn (for which we hired him), or in employing the wrong means (e.g. using tiny pieces rather than boards, or nails rather than screws), would we seek, as the missing reason, *his* rule of procedure, viz. 'Why are you doing *that*?' or 'Why are you doing it *that way*?', in which case his explanation might be, in the first case, 'Because your wife asked me', or in the second case, 'Because this is the traditional method of cabinet making in my family'.

In sum, giving reasons for actions is citing goals and/or means–ends rules for achieving goals. What then is their connection with desires, feelings and emotions?

## *The Role of Wants, Desires and Feelings*

Wanting, as we saw in the previous chapter, is a catch-all motivational term that indicates that the action it modifies is voluntary and either not in need of reasons ('Because I want to'), or a means to some desired goal ('Because I want G and doing A is the way to get G'), or that the agent is in some determinable state requiring action, the determinate state being specifiable as desire, need, craving, longing, compulsion, temptation, etc.

While more specific than 'want', 'desire' is still both vague and ambiguous (even more so in French, where '*désirer*' is practically synonymous with '*vouloir*'). But 'desire' is more suggestive of agitation, feeling and reduced control than 'want', although less so than 'crave' or 'long for'. We speak more easily of desires as irresistible than of wants, while craving and need entail (*ceteris paribus*) irresistibility, and longing entails both irresistibility and unattainability of its object. Unlike wanting, which is seldom felt, we *feel* our desires, cravings and longings. Needs are more complex. One may feel a need that one does not really have, or not feel one (not even be aware of one) that one does really have. Needs can be subjective or objective, illusory or real, conscious or unconscious. This is also true of wants, so that one can say, on occasion, 'You don't *really* want that, you only think you do'.[7] Not so for desires, cravings, etc. Psychoanalytic talk of unconscious desires and wishes is poor choice of language. 'Unconscious needs and wants' would be better English for the message of psychoanalytic theory. The main difference between need and want is evaluative. To say that X needs O is, to some extent, to express approval of X's having O.[8] Not so for wanting, except in that somewhat archaic usage as synonymous with lack, as in Robert Burns's 'Some have meat but cannot eat, and some that can, they want it'.

Confining the discussion to desires, let us examine their relation to feelings. Feelings, I suggest, are precisely what William James mistook emotions to be, namely, awareness of bodily agitations. What kind of awareness? The thesis of Chapter 2 on avowals suggested that feelings (which, together with preferences, intentions and beliefs, are prime objects of avowals) are not entirely passive, but are interpretive and evaluative responses to a situation that includes one's own bodily changes. A throb of remorse, or of fear, or of envy or of joy, as Ryle pointed out, is just the same throb, physiologically. The difference among them consists in what they signify to the subject who feels them, that is, in whether he regards the situation he is in as good or bad, and in his *reasons* for so regarding it (e.g. having done something wrong, facing danger, seeing another succeed where he has failed, or achieving a desired goal, respectively). So we see that even feelings essentially involve reasons. And only when one's reasons for his feelings are foolish are his feelings irrational. It is an almost ubiquitous error of psychologists and philosophers to have relegated emotions, desires and feelings to the realm of the non-rational. The probable source of the mistake is that 'affective states' are less under one's control than are one's thoughts, assertions and actions, and therefore somewhat less subject to commendation or condemnation as wise or foolish, admirable or culpable. But as Thomas Nagel has cogently argued in his recent book, *The Possibility of Altruism*,[9] affective states are not entirely immune to criticism, nor to one's voluntary control, since they are grounded on beliefs and values that are subject to rational attack and defence.

Now as to desires – how do they differ from feelings? For one thing, desires are intentional, they are desires *for* such and such, whereas feelings are, one might say, only quasi-intentional, that is, they are feelings *of* – not external objects, but one's own states, such as pain, pleasure, remorse, joy, etc. We feel our own emotions and desires, but the latter, while often the objects of our feelings, are not themselves feelings, on pain of infinite regress, nor, as Kenny and T. Nagel have shown, do they entail feelings as necessary criteria for their existence. I must be *aware* of a desire in order to have it, but I need not *feel* it (although one usually feels something related to the desire, e.g. when one desires food, one usually feels hunger; when he desires power, he feels envy toward those who have it, etc.). Desire for wealth, fame, and other abstract conditions is seldom attended by sufficient neural agitation and consequent sensation to be felt. Sensual desires are, of course, always felt, or they wouldn't be sensual. As for emotions, we shall see later that they need not be felt nor (unlike desires) need we even be aware of them (although non-awareness of one's emotions is pathological).

The important difference between feelings and desires, a difference which explains the grammatical point just made, is that desires motivate, while feelings alone do not. *Ceteris paribus*, if we want or desire G, we set out to get it. Thus desires help to explain actions by indicating the goals to which the actions are means, although as T. Nagel has shown, desires are not *necessary* elements of action explanations, since the very reasons that motivate desire may also motivate action without the intervention of desire (as in long-range prudential actions like saving money, or morally governed actions like refusing a bribe).

EMOTION

In his chapter on emotion in *The Concept of Mind*, Ryle brought attention to the complexity of this concept by analysing it into four components: inclination, agitation, feeling and mood, and thus as a rather canine family of 'mongrel categoricals'. Although Ryle dug beneath the simplistic tendency of introspective psychologists to identify emotion with feeling, and the equally simplistic identification of emotion with neural tension perpetrated by physiological psychologists,[10] and even by Freud in his more reductionist moods, he still barely scratched the surface.[11] Ryle failed to take note of an essential component of the meaning of emotion terms, namely, their dual evaluation function: (1) in indicating the subject's evaluation of his situation and (2) in expressing the speaker's evaluation of the subject's response as when we describe a person as over-anxious, or panicky, or envious. This crucial oversight was first brought to light by Errol Bedford, in an illuminating essay, 'Emotions'.[12] To Bedford's sound criticism I would add that Ryle, like most psychologists, also did insufficient justice to the *intentional* character of emotions, i.e. the fact that they are responses to (real or imagined) objects, events or states. There are of course some generalised and apparently non-directed emotions such as vague anxiety, Kafkian guilt, and euphoria. Existential philosophers such as Kierkegaard, Heidegger, Jaspers and Sartre suggest that these generalised emotions do have an object, but a very special one: God, for Kierkegaard and Jaspers, Being for Heidegger and Sartre. Freud ascribed to them more mundane objects (parents) awareness of which is repressed into the unconscious. Since I have no idea of how God or Being can be an *object*, Freud seems to me to have offered the only account supported by clinical (or any other kind of) evidence. Nonetheless, even if Freud is right about the initial etiology of such apparently objectless emotions, there would seem to be no inconsistency in regarding them as directed not toward a definite object, but toward an indefinite object. Anxiety, for instance, while it is not fear of anything definite, such as parental punishment or social ostracism or insects, etc., might well be fear of just plain *something*, or *that* something bad will happen to one. In any case, these diffuse emotions are very special cases that we may leave to psychiatrists, whether Freudian or existentialist, to inform us more about, while we concentrate on the more usual and paradigmatic types of emotions.

But before terminating this digression and returning to our main theme, it may be worth noting that Sartre's perceptive account of emotions, in his early monograph on that subject, was seriously marred by his reliance both on scientific psychology and on *Existenz Philosophie*. Like many psychologists (e.g. Duffy, op. cit.), Sartre assumed emotions to be an irrational escape from reality and, going beyond even Heidegger and Jaspers, he defined *all* emotions as directed toward Being, namely, as 'magical transformation of the world'.[13] One must go back to Aristotle, Aquinas and Spinoza to be reminded of the simple fact that emotions are usually rationally grounded and useful to us, and that without emotion, life would neither be long-lived, nor worth the long-living.

But now to return to the main issue: what sort of states are emotions, and how are they related to reasons and to feelings? I have already noted, following Kenny and Bedford, that while emotion predicates usually involve dispositions toward certain feelings (e.g. 'jealous' *suggests*, but does not entail, that the subject will feel throbs, pangs, or sundry sensations when, say, he notices his wife flirting with another man) such feelings are not essential to emotions. We know, for example, that Stalin was jealous of Trotsky's intellectual superiority, without having the least idea of Stalin's feelings, nor indeed any assurance that Stalin had *any* feelings about Trotsky. What seems beyond doubt is that Stalin was not constantly experiencing throbs or pangs at the thought of Trotsky throughout the twenty-odd years of their rivalry, although he was, throughout that period, jealous enough to make frequent efforts to have Trotsky assassinated.

The connection between emotions and feelings is, I think, similar to that described by T. Nagel's account of the connection between desires and actions, namely, that both are motivated by the same reasons and thus related through a common ground. One's reason for being jealous toward his wife is[14] that she may be unfaithful to him, and that is precisely his reason for *feeling* throbs, twinges or pangs of jealousy when she goes off on a journey alone, or when he observes her flirting. Whether or not our subject actually feels throbs, twinges or pangs would, I should imagine, depend on how excitable his neuro-endocrinological system happens to be. Stalin was not an excitable man; neither was he a man of intense feelings. A man who neither shows nor avows (even to himself) intense feelings does not, so far as I can understand the concept, *have* intense feelings. But insofar as he does have and manifests such feelings, they are associated with emotions through their common ground of reasons.

How then are emotions grounded on reasons? Again, I shall rely on T. Nagel's helpful discussion. Reasons, I have argued, are premisses for practical reasoning that guides action – they are reasons for doing, not just feeling, so that one may, conceivably, act on one's reasons without experiencing either emotion or feelings, although I would imagine that such cases are pathological and rare, and that people who frequently act unemotionally are not the best friends to have – they are the kind of heartless bureaucrats who can order mass bombings of defenceless populations for 'reasons of state'.[15] In this respect, I think Nagel's account of moral action is too strictly Kantian and erroneously discounts the role of moral emotions (e.g. Hume's sentiment of 'benevolence') that serve to limit mechanical obedience to general rules of action. For example, the soldiers of Company C at My Lai, who fired in the air or refused to fire at all, were deterred from acting on the rule of military obedience by their emotions of pity and horror at the prospect of the slaughter of innocents. Does this mean that these emotions were irrational, i.e. not grounded on reasons? Of course not, but the reason that motivated them, namely, the rule that one ought not to slaughter the defenceless, could only prevail over the rule of military obedience with the help of the emotions of pity and horror.

But now, in maintaining that emotions can motivate exceptions to rules, as well as that reasons as rules direct action and restrain emotions, have I not returned after all to the traditional Platonic–Cartesian split between reason and emotion, despite my initial claim that they are interconnected? It looks this way, but the looks are deceiving. The resolution of this apparent inconsistency may be found in the recognition of the *dispositional* component of the meaning of emotion predicates, a component I argued for in the section on motives in the preceding chapter. It is not enough to say that both emotions and actions are grounded on or motivated by reasons. Unlike all but the most habitual actions, emotions involve, among other things, tendencies toward certain kinds of responses. As Ryle pointed out, the frustration of a tendency produces neural agitation, thus accounting for the fact that we so often, although not always, feel our emotions. The tendency component of emotion makes it possible for the agent to refrain from acting on a reason that directs behaviour contrary to the tendency involved, and thus provides a kind of scale for weighing competing reasons.

Thus to say that X is angry at Y, or jealous of Z, or in love with W, is not *merely* (as Ryle too often suggests) to attribute to X inclinations toward certain open-ended ranges of behaviour and avowal, but it surely is *in part* to do just that. The main additional components that Ryle overlooked are the intentionality of emotions and the normative assessments they express, both of which lead us back to reasons. X cannot be angry at Y without any reason, real or fancied, provided by Y; X must at least believe that Y has wronged him. Nor can X be jealous or in love unless the object of his emotion has, or seems to have, features that, for him, justify the kind of behaviour characteristic of these emotions.

In what way then can emotions inhibit or support reasons for actions rather than merely epiphenomenally reflecting such reasons, as Nagel seems to hold? My suggestion is this: an emotion is a tendency to weigh certain reasons above others in accordance with one's beliefs and values and in relation to a given situation. To ascribe an emotion to oneself or to another person is, above all, to provide information about one's own or another's scale of values. Our emotions, which manifest the relative weight we assign to reasons for action, distinguish us as unique individuals, while our intellectual and moral judgments stem from our common human nature, i.e. from our common ability to recognise and respect reasons. There are, of course, limits to the individual variability of emotions, particularly in the case of the distinctly moral emotions such as sympathy, pity, loyalty, gratitude, etc. for these are (ideally, if not in fact) evoked in all to the same degree by the same situations. But this is, at best, true only in simple situations where only one such emotion is appropriate. More often, they come into conflict, the resolution of which then varies with the individual. Where love of one's family motivates disloyalty to one's political party or nation, it would be callous to denounce the victim of so agonising a conflict of values, no matter which way he resolves it. Sartre wisely declined to advise a young Frenchman who faced a choice between fighting in the Resistance and taking care of his dependent mother. Insofar as patriotism and filial love qualify as emotions, two individuals will differ in the degree to which they are moved more by the one than by the other, with respect to the particular objects of these emotions.

To sum up our findings, it is misleading to think of emotions as states of either psychic or neural agitation, or as irrational responses to disturbing situations. To attribute an emotion like anger, love or jealousy to oneself or to another is to explain his present and likely future actions in terms of the way he envisions his situation, the way he interprets his bodily agitations (if any), the goals he pursues, the relative values he places on those goals, and the rules of action that, for him, link means and ends. In brief, ascribing an emotion to a person is short-hand for an extraordinary amount of information about him, which may help explain why adequate psychological understanding is so difficult to achieve.

It is of course very tempting to visualise emotions as causal forces, as neural or psychic 'springs of action' that push us or pull us, impel or propel us into action, on the assumption that human actions, like natural events, are to be explained by antecedent causes. This temptation, due to our penchant for causal explanation, is further intensified by the frequent attendance of emotions by bodily agitations, and the phenomenological fact that, when in an intensely emotional state, we usually feel impelled by some inner force that is not within our rational control.

But if we are to understand psychological discourse in a clear enough way to formulate adequately subtle criteria of verification, we must recognise this way of thinking to be metaphorical and misleading (overemphasising, as it does, the pathological cases of emotion as against the normal cases) and, like good phenomenological psychiatrists, attempt to discover a person's *reasons* for his emotions and actions, rather than *blocking* explanations with: 'Poor chap, he just can't help himself, he's driven' (by what? an internal piston, a demon, an irresistible psychic push or a neural explosion?),[16] a causal model that will get us nowhere in understanding ourselves and others.

H. Mullane has maintained[17] that the unconscious reasons of a psychopathic person are not 'his' reasons[18] but are somehow imposed upon him by some causal process that Mullane suggests may be 'neurophysiological.'[19] Such reasons are therefore 'non-rational' reasons. The very notion of non-rational reasons strikes one as unnecessarily paradoxical. Mullane wants to explain why compulsive behaviour is to some degree excusable without justifying it as rational, even from the standpoint of the agent's beliefs. I have already indicated, in the discussion of Dray and Peters in the preceding chapter, how we can avoid such absurd relativism of justification without paying Mullane's price of non-rational causal explanation. To revert to causes, whether psychic or neurological, exculpates *completely*, and this is a consequence that Mullaney himself recognises, toward the end of his essay, and then tries desperately to escape by weakening his deterministic account of compulsive behaviour, thereby throwing in the sponge: 'It is only the *general* neurotic pattern of behaviour that can be legitimately taken as caused by unconscious processes over which the agent has no control.'[20]

A simpler way out of the difficulty Mullane rightly points to, of *partially* excusing neurotic behaviour while still explaining it in terms of reasons (bad reasons, yet not bad because of ignorance but bad because of deliberate self-deception (see Chapter 7)), is that 'psychic compulsion' is a metaphor for the natural tendency to avoid suffering. If a kleptomaniac finds relief from frustration, guilt or a sense of impotence by stealing, we pity him enough to assign him therapy rather than punishment, as we do (or should do) for a narcotic addict, without having to deny that he did, voluntarily, steal or take dope. The therapy should aim at helping the agent to find more acceptable and less self-destructive ways of satisfying his needs, thereby reshaping his values and goals into a more 'integrated' (i.e. rational) structure. But again, there is no necessity to drag causality back into the explanatory picture.

# 5 The Incoherence of Determinism

'No supposition seems to me more natural than that there is no process in the brain correlated with . . . thinking; so that it would be impossible to read off thought-processes from brain processes' – Wittgenstein, *Zettel*

'Why should there not be a psychological regularity to which *no* physiological regularity corresponds? If this upsets our concept of causality then it is high time it was upset' – Ibid.

I have been trying to show how and why causal explanation is inappropriate to human action, whose explanation has a different structure and does a different job from that of scientific laws and theories. Now if what has so far been maintained is correct in the main (even assuming errors of detail), does it then follow that man introduces an element of indeterminism into nature, a causally inexplicable break in the chain of law-like regularities, or can causal determinism still co-exist peacefully with action discourse, as most philosophers have maintained? I shall argue here that the main accounts of the relation between mind and body relied on to support the compatibility of causal determinism with psychological explanation of voluntary action are, to the degree they are clear, clearly inconsistent.

## THE IRRELEVANCE DEFENCE

Professor A. I. Melden, whose pioneer work, *Free Action*, has been one of the main sources of inspiration for the present study, draws back from the edge of indeterminism after leading his reader to that edge:

Does the rejection of the causal model imply that actions are uncaused, that freedom is to be purchased at the expense of a capricious indeterminism, or of a libertarianism that misrepresents every responsible action as an heroic effort that somehow thwarts the causal order? Quite the contrary, the argument is designed to show the logical incoherence involved in the supposition that actions, desires, intentions, etc. stand in causal relations . . .[1]

Disregarding the rather gratuitous epithet 'capricious' that Melden inserts in front of 'indeterminism', it is very hard to see how the claim, at the end of the above passage, that it is incoherent to suppose that actions, etc. stand in causal relations is 'the contrary' of the claim that actions break the causal chains of nature. When Melden traces a causal chain involving action, he does not find a break, not because the break isn't there, but because he changes direction just before he reaches it, as if sensing that he is approaching the edge of a chasm. In Chapter 6 of *Free Action*, Melden traces the physiological causal sequence whereby, when one raises his arm, the motion of the arm is caused by muscular contractions that in turn are caused by efferent neural impulses from the brain. The obvious next question, which Melden does not ask, is this: What, if anything, causes those efferent impulses from brain to muscles, which produce, as their effect, the very event that *I* perform as my action of raising my arm? Now either these efferent impulses were in turn caused by certain afferent impulses from sensory organs affected by external stimuli, or by the combination of such afferent signals with modulating processes within the brain (such modulating processes in turn having been caused by physical events external to the brain, such as past conditioning), or they simply were not caused at all but only 'brought about' and 'employed' by the agent in performing the action for which the efferent impulses are necessary and sufficient conditions. But Melden does not ask this further question, and so, of course he does not have to answer it. As far as I know, *no one* has asked the precise question: Can we fully explain our brain activity in terms of antecedent conditions and laws without reference to what we are doing? Yet the question stands there grinning at us, like Austin's frog at the bottom of the beer mug, challenging us to face and answer it. For if the answer is affirmative, then the concept of voluntary action and the entire mode of discourse resting on it becomes a kind of mythological luxury, appealed to only when we are ignorant of the remote causal conditions. If the answer is negative, then the locus of physical indeterminism, the gap in the causal chain of nature, has been pinpointed, namely, the human brain. By this I mean that some modulating synapses are set off in the brain *by the fact that we do certain things*, such as raising our arms. If for some reason I wanted to bring about the brain events $B_n$ that cause my arm to rise, I could do it by raising my arm.[2] In this case, the later event, the action, is the means and the earlier brain events are the end. Normally, it is the other way around. Can we then be said to *cause* our brain events $B_n$, in that we *bring them about* in raising our arm? If so, then we have the temporal anomaly of the cause (the *act* of raising one's arm) occurring later than its effect (brain events $B_n$).[3] I see no harm in speaking this way, but on the other hand, there seems no reason why we must. This only goes to show that the notion of an agent's *bringing*

*about* an event, while it involves causation, is too complex to be reduced
to causal chains alone, since it also involves the purposive relation of
means–end which, as we have seen, sometimes goes backwards in time.

The attempts of action theorists like Melden to avoid indeterminism
by appealing to the semantic irrelevance of causal language to action,
from which appeal, by a *non sequitur*, they conclude that causal and
action explanations are independent and thus compatible, founders on
the fact that every action is identical with some physical event, namely,
a movement of the agent's body. The same *event* is an action under one
*description* and a physical motion under another description (e.g. raising
one's hand *vis-à-vis* one's hand rising). Now if all physical motions were
determined by antecedent causes, then it would follow that actions,
which are, under another description, the same events as certain
physical motions, are equally determined by antecedent causes. More
accurately, to avoid misunderstanding, the *event E* which, under an
action description is A, but under a motion description is M, is determined by antecedent causes. The fact that it is semantically anomalous
to ascribe a cause to E *as A* does not, *contra* Ryle and Melden, dissolve
the issue of determinism versus indeterminism, nor weigh in favour of
the former, for the following question remains in need of a straight
answer: Is E *as M* determined by antecedent causes or not? *This*
question, surely, is semantically *kosher*. Yet if its correct answer is
affirmative, then it is hair-splitting to refuse to admit that actions are
causally explicable. Now, if we are to deny this consequence, then, by
*modus tollens*, we must also deny its first hypothesis, namely, that all
physical events are determined by antecedent causes, or else its second
hypothesis, namely, that actions are the same *events* as bodily motions
although their descriptions differ in explanatory richness (action
description including reference to conventions, rules, reasons, etc.).
And surely the second hypothesis is less doubtful than the first. For to
deny *it* is to claim, either that actions are not observable events, or
that there are observable events that are not physical events, and either
of these claims gets us into worse trouble than admitting indeterminism.

THE DUALISTIC INTERACTION DEFENCE

The unsatisfactory efforts of conceptual dualism (of the kind just
described) to avoid the embarrassing consequences of indeterminism
may (and often do) incline philosophers back toward traditional (i.e.
substantial) dualism, which at least offers a straightforward affirmative
answer to the question: Are all events, including human actions,
causally determined? The spelling out of this answer consists in the
doctrine usually called 'interactionism', whose technical formulation

began with Descartes,[4] although it has always been implicit in common-sense attitudes that take spiritualism, magic and occult phenomena seriously. On this view, some physical causes produce mental events such as motives, intentions and volitions, and these mental events in turn produce bodily movements as actions. Thus there need be no breaks in the causal chains of nature, provided that we recognise mental events as some of the links in some chains. Free or voluntary action is defined, on this dualist 'soft-determinist' view, as action that is mediated by such mental events as intentions and volitions, without the latter being exempted from having antecedent causes themselves. As indicated in the previous chapters, this view has been the target of Wittgenstein and post-Wittgensteinian philosophers, and is now so riddled with holes that lapsing back to it to justify determinism is hardly worth the high price in incoherence. For, as all the writers I have cited have argued, if this view were true, then voluntary action would be just as illusory as on the hypothesis of purely physical determinism. If a mental event called 'motive' (or 'intention' or whatever it is called) is produced in my mind by an external cause independently of my wanting it to occur, then it is not *my* motive or intention, since *I* have not brought it about. It is 'mine' only in the weaker sense that a bruise on my leg is my bruise, i.e. it is something that has happened to me, but not something that I have willed, or done, and therefore not mine in the more intimate sense of 'mine' that voluntariness entails. But if the cause is not mine in that sense, then neither is its inevitable effect – the movement of my body. Consequently, the movement that such an externally produced 'intention' or 'motive' causes is not *my action*, but simply an event in the course of nature. But if voluntary action on this view turns out to be illusory in this way, then the dualist theory resorted to in order to reconcile freedom with determinism has jettisoned precisely what it was designed to rescue.

I shall put the matter in the form of a visualisable analogy which may show how easy a step it is from dualism to physical reductionism. The deterministic interactionist theory we are considering conceives of intentions, desires and motives as sufficient conditions for voluntary actions which are in turn determined by external causes or stimuli. To act freely, on this view, is to perform an action that is determined by a mental cause, such as an intention or motive or desire, and this mental cause is itself an effect of some external physical cause. The visualisable model I want to suggest is an electric circuit consisting of a battery as source of energy, a buzzer which is activated when the circuit is closed, a button that anyone may push for the purpose of ringing the buzzer, and a *soi-disant* 'switch' or circuit-breaker, which is so connected to the button by a rigid bar, that when the button is depressed the 'switch' is depressed with it, thus closing the circuit. The point I want to make about the 'switch' is that it may look like a switch, and we may call it a switch, but it isn't doing the job of a switch, which is to *prevent* the circuit from being closed by mere pressing of the button by some unauthorised person. Imagine that the switch is inside a locked cabinet, so that no one but the owner of the key can directly press the handle of the 'switch', although anyone who presses the button will automatically cause the switch to close. If this system seems silly, so much the better – that precisely is the moral I wish to draw. The system may be illustrated as follows:

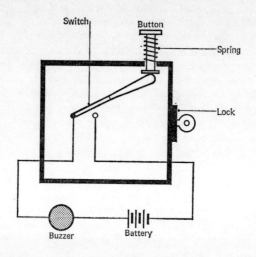

Now I suggest that the dualistic determinist thinks of intentions, desires and motives on the model of the above diagram, as automatically activated or brought about by external causes and, in doing so, renders them as unnecessary and pointless as the 'switch' in the diagram. A 'switch' that automatically closes is not, as the ancients would say, a *vera causa*, but a spurious, epiphenomenal 'cause', since it would be misleading to say that the closing of the switch was the cause of the buzzer sounding, rather than the depressing of the button, just as it would be misleading, as Mill observed, to call night the cause of day.[5]

The situation being envisaged is something like that of a lock on a door that automatically opens when the doorknob is turned. A lock that doesn't keep anyone out is like a circuit-breaking switch that doesn't prevent current from flowing. Now on the dualistic soft-determinist view, an agent's motive is produced by external causes. If so, it will no more serve to restrain the agent's action than our silly 'switch' will prevent the buzzer from sounding. This, I suggest, is what William James was driving at, in 'The Dilemma of Determinism', when he characterised soft determinism as a 'hoax' on the ground that it offers us desires and motives as epiphenomenal pseudo-causes and tells us that we are 'free'.

But the diagram above may be helpful in illustrating an important fact about voluntary action. While *motives* are wrongly pictured as switches, there is something else that can be so pictured, namely, the modulating processes in the brain to which I referred earlier in this chapter. These are processes that mediate between physical stimuli and behavioural responses, and with which materialists are often tempted to identify motives, because such processes are necessary conditions for voluntary actions, as distinct from reflexes. The reader may recall that I raised the question: What brings about such modulating brain processes – external stimulation alone, or the agent himself? My answer was that *the agent's action* brings about the very process that is temporally followed by the action and is necessary for performing the action. The relation between human action and brain processes is therefore contra-causal, and the brain processes involved are indeterminate events. *We* bring them about, in acting, but nothing causes them to occur.

THE IDENTITY DEFENCE

The diagram just considered reveals the close affinity between dualistic determinism and physical reductionism, the only difference being that the 'switch' in question is an immaterial 'mental' one for the dualist and a brain process for the physical reductionist. It is bad enough for our 'switch' to be a pseudo-switch on either view, but the dualist position further suffers from all the faults of negative theology in that it is parasitic on metaphors borrowed from physicalism. Thus, if it has any merit, that merit belongs more to the view on which it feeds according to which, motives and other psychological states or processes are identical with bodily processes. I shall now argue that all variants of this mind-body identity theory are as incoherent, if more subtly so, as the dualistic view we have considered.

The most popular solution to the 'mind-body problem' seems to be the theory of 'extensional identity', according to which descriptions of mental states and descriptions of certain physiological states (usually brain states) are different descriptions of the same entities.[6] On this view, while we can say certain things about mental states that we cannot say about bodily states and vice versa (e.g. a certain thought may be clever, but not its corresponding bodily state, a sensation may be blue, but not a brain process, etc.), the entity satisfying a mentalist description also satisfies some physiological description, just as one and the same entity satisfies the two descriptions 'ray of light' and 'electromagnetic wave', although it takes different predicates under each description, e.g. a ray of light may be bright, a wave may have a certain frequency, but not vice versa.

I shall argue that this type of 'solution' to the mind-body problem is mathematically impossible. If two sets, A and B, are co-extensive (have the same members), then they can be mapped in one-to-one correspondence, i.e. every element of A can be matched with exactly one element of B and conversely. This relation is, of course, reflexive, that is, every set is co-extensive with itself. Now the number of possible mental states of a thinking organism is, I shall argue, infinite, while the the number of possible bodily states of that organism is necessarily finite. Consequently, the set of possible mental states of an organism cannot be matched one-to-one with the set of possible bodily states. Still less, then, can the two sets have identical elements.

To see that the number of *possible* mental states of any thinking organism is infinite,[7] let us simplify matters by considering just a subset of the set of all mental states, namely, the set of thoughts of natural numbers. There must be just as many *possible* thoughts of natural numbers as there are natural numbers, since there is no reason why a thinking organism (who knows arithmetic) cannot think of any particular number. Now the set of natural numbers is infinite. So, then, must be the set of thoughts that it is possible for an arithmetically literate organism to think. We can identify thoughts of natural numbers by correlating them with the numbers they are thoughts of, so that the thought of 1 is $T_1$, the thought of 2 is $T_2$, and the thought of any number is $T_n$. Then the cardinal number of $\{T_n\}$ is aleph null.

Now consider the bodily states that may be claimed to be identical with mental states. The usual candidates nowadays are firings of neurons in the brain cells. Now the number of neurons in any brain is necessarily finite, although, of course, very large. Let us assign to the largest brain that ever will exist the number of neurons K. The number of combinations of neuron firings would then be $2^k$. Since K is finite, so is $2^k$. Thus there are more thoughts thinkable by a rational organism than there are brain states to match with those thoughts. Suppose teams of physiological psychologists worked for millions of years, matching thoughts of numbers as reported by subjects with their brain states as identified by encephalograms. When they have completed $2^k$ successful matchings, their supply of brain states would have run out. Yet clearly, their subjects could go on thinking of natural numbers previously unthought. Now either their new thoughts would occur without any brain state occurring (which is, of course, highly unlikely), or they would have to use brain states that had already been used for previous thoughts. In brief, the relation between thoughts and brain states cannot be one–one, or one–many, as identity theorists claim (cf. Feigl), but must rather be many–many. The interesting further consequence follows that thoughts cannot be determined by bodily states alone; the latter may be necessary conditions for the former, but they cannot be sufficient conditions, since the same brain state may be used to think more than one (indeed, an infinite number of) thoughts.[8]

OBJECTIONS AND REPLIES

*Objection one*
It may be argued, as Professor Feigl has argued in correspondence with me, that my reasoning involves an equivocation between any and all. I have said that a mind can think of any natural number, but my refutation of mind–body identity requires the assumption that a mind can think of *all* numbers, while brain states, being finite in number cannot represent all numbers, but only any finite set of numbers.

'Given an efficient notation (in terms of exponents, etc.) a brain – or a computer – might indeed have the capacity for tokening any natural number (i.e. any one), but it is surely asking for something logically impossible to have it token *all* (i.e. *every*) natural numbers within a finite time. Given infinite time I am sure that some device like exponentiation would enable the brain to token the infinite sequence of natural numbers. Ask yourself how you would produce thoughts of tremendously large numbers – you may very well have to admit that even "pure thoughts" could only represent these numbers – either by the trivial "plus one" gimmick, or else by an abbreviatorily powerful notation.'[9]

Have I committed an any-all equivocation? I think not. It is not essential to my argument that an organism (or mind) be able to think of all numbers – it is essential only that he be able to think of any of the infinite set of natural numbers. The point is that, if all the $2^k$ brain states be correlated one to one with thoughts of numbers from 1 to $2^k$, there will be no brain states left to correlate with (i.e. on identity theory, to *be*) thoughts of numbers greater than $2^k$. Professor Feigl's point about exponentiation does not, I think, help us here, because all that exponentiation can do is to abbreviate the physical representation of numbers – it cannot magically produce an infinite set out of a finite set. If brain states be correlated with thoughts, then of course certain brain states, $B_m$, will be correlated with exponential thoughts. But the fact remains that there are exactly $2^k$ brain states, so that, while some of the $2^k$ states will be exponential thoughts, and others will be non-exponential thoughts, there will still be none left to be identical with thoughts of numbers greater than $2^k$. This objection is a more sophisticated form of the one which I dismissed in my previous footnote on grounds of irrelevance.

*Objection two*

It may be objected that I have assumed without warrant a discrete state theory of brain activity, and that there are other theories, such as that of Wolfgang Koehler, according to which thought is produced by an electrical field in the brain. Since a field is continuous, it may be that each thought should be correlated, not with the firing of discrete neurons, but with a dimensionless point of the electrical field. Since the number of such points is aleph one, there are enough such brain states to accommodate thoughts of any numbers.[10] My reply to this objection is that dimensionless points are not physical states of a brain, they are mathematical idealisations of physical states. I do not deny that it is possible to correlate all mental states with numbers or geometrical points. I mean to deny only that all mental states can be correlated with genuine bodily states. A bodily state must, by the meaning of 'body' occupy a non-zero three-dimensional space. So this resort to Platonism will not do as a defence of materialistic reductionism.

In a series of papers on minds and computers,[11] Hilary Putnam has developed an account of mental predicates as 'logical' or 'functional' states of 'probabilistic automata', an account that seems to provide sophisticated support for identity theory, even though Putnam himself expresses some doubt about this. However, his doubts are empirical rather than semantical; they are doubts that 'functional states' and brain states *will* be correlated, not that they *could* be correlated. Bruce Aune has rightly commented that 'Putnam's sympathies still seem to lie with the idea that the empirical features of the functional states ... will be physical'.[12]

Now it seems to me that both Putnam and Aune are victims of a type-token confusion in even considering it possible that logical or functional relations (the term 'state' seems to me inappropriate for logical or functional entities for precisely this reason, namely, that it conflates the abstract entity with the token that represents it – only the latter can be a state or a process) could be correlated with physical states. Putnam explains functional states in terms of program instructions on a machine tape. But the marks on a tape are neither logical nor functional entities; they are merely the physical vehicles or symbols of logical functions. And where are the logical functions? Clearly they are nowhere but in the mind of the operator of the computer; surely they are not in the computer itself. Thus there can be no question of correlating the logical or functional 'states' of a machine with its physical states.

I can think of no other objections to my argument than those already considered which is, of course, no guarantee that there are none. But I have posed this argument to many colleagues and have heard no rejoinders other than the above which, for the reasons given, I do not find persuasive.

Saul Kripke has advanced an interesting argument against mind–body identity which adds support to the thesis of this chapter.[18] Kripke argues that if what are taken at first to be two entities denoted by 'rigid designators' (i.e. expressions having a necessarily fixed reference) are found to be in fact identical, then their identity reduces to self-identity which is a necessary relation so that the assertion of their identity is a necessary truth even though it has been discovered *a-posteriori*. He maintains that expressions denoting mental states like pains or thoughts are rigid designators, and so he claims are descriptions of brain states such as the excitation of C-fibres. Consequently, if the two types of things are in fact identical, the assertion of their identity would be a necessary truth as, for example, the identity of light with electro-magnetic waves, or heat with molecular motion. Yet the identity of mental states with brain states is not claimed to be a necessary truth, for the good reason that we can so easily conceive it to be not true at all.

There are ambiguities in Kripke's account which it may be instructive to examine closely. He seems to shift from a correct insight about identity of particulars as denoted by proper names to a doubtful claim about identity of types of things as denoted by common nouns and descriptions. He maintains, mistakenly I think, that sortal nouns like 'tiger', mass nouns like 'gold' and other natural kind nouns are rigid designators similar to proper names, which seems to imply the Aristotelian view that species are abstract entities distinct from their identifying properties. This degree of ontological realism seems unnecessarily extravagant. Consider Kripke's favourite example, the noun 'gold'. He maintains that the reference of 'gold' is rigidly fixed, consisting in paradigm specimens of gold. Yet he concedes that it is both logically and empirically possible that all that glitters in Fort Knox and on the Gold Exchange might turn out to be only 'fool's gold' or iron pyrite. Were this found to be the case, we would no longer identify such worthless dross as gold. We would conclude that true gold is not to be found on earth but perhaps on some other planet. A crash programme might be instituted for developing commercial rockets for a celestial gold rush. The serious point is that there is no way to distinguish the reference of a common noun from our paradigm specimens of it, and since the latter are subject to correction, the denotation cannot be fixed with absolute rigidity. Moreover, when we teach the use of common nouns, we do so by indicating properties rather than substances. For example, when teaching a small child to use 'cow', we usually show him a picture of a cow rather than dragging him off to a dairy farm. The picture obviously does not fix the reference, but only manifests the properties of bovinity.

The reason for Kripke's ontological extravagance may lie in the fact that he so often has mathematical examples in mind. In mathematics, designators like numerals are rigid in a quite different way from that in which proper names are rigid, so that the syntactical analogy on which Kripke relies is misleading. Mathematical expressions are strictly governed in their reference by rules and postulates, so that it is by stipulation that we assign to a numeral a unique reference. In brief, the reference of a mathematical expression is determined *a-priori*, while that of a proper name is determined by the act of naming on acquaintance with the object. In contrast with both of these procedures, the reference of common nouns denoting natural kinds is partially fixed by selection of paradigm instances, but these paradigms are assumed to share one or more essential properties and, in case they do not, the common noun in question no longer designates them.

For these reasons it is important to keep separate and distinct the problems of particular identity from those of type identity. The former is a necessary condition, but not a sufficient condition for the latter. Now Kripke is right to hold that a *particular* mental state cannot be identical with a *particular* brain state on the ground that such identity would have to be necessary and clearly is not. And from the non-identity of particular instances he might then have deduced the non-identity of the types of which they are instances. But his mistake was to tackle identity of types directly, in terms of the doubtful concept of rigid designation as applied to both concrete and abstract entities, which raises more problems than it solves.

Moreover, the mathematical argument sketched earlier is, I think, on firmer grounds than Kripke's argument, for the latter assumes that we can demonstratively indicate a pain on the one hand and a brain state on the other. Now it is at least very doubtful whether it even makes sense to try to indicate a pain demonstratively. How would we go about doing this? We cannot point to our mental states. I can speak of 'the pain I feel now', but in what way is such a speech act like a baptismal ritual? To believe it is, is to make two mistakes: (1) to commit the fallacy noted by Ryle of assimilating sensation to observation and (2) to assume that mental states are *bona fide* entities. I have argued throughout that psychological predicates do not designate entities, but provide evaluative explanations of circumstances, bodily states and reasons for action.

It may appear to the reader that my mathematical argument against identity theories presupposes that thoughts are countable entities that could conceivably, if not in fact, be paired off with brain states. But such a reading would miss the main thrust of my discussion, which is, after *supposing* (just to give the devil his due) that thoughts are countable entities, and then showing that, even if they were, there would be more thoughts than brain states, to support the very different conception of a thought as the *use* a person makes of any object including states of his own body, to convey meaning. This is why there are more thoughts than physical objects, for any physical object (or type of object) can be put to a limitless number of different designative uses, e.g. the numeral '1' can be used to designate the number one, the number one million, a gram of weight or the winner of a tournament. To paraphrase Wittgenstein, a thought is the meaning of a sign, and the meaning is its use.

Thus I do not intend the argument to lead us back to the metaphysical dualism from which Wittgenstein and Ryle have liberated us. Quite the contrary; the argument, in establishing that thoughts cannot be the *same* entities as brain states in no way entails that they are entities of any sort. The argument supports, rather than undermines, the general claim of this study that psychological terms are not primarily referential in their linguistic function, but explanatory and evaluative. To say that someone has a thought is to say that he is making a reasonably intelligent use of a sign. To say that he feels pain is to say that he is in a state that he judges to be undesirable.

It was necessary to digress into the mind–body issue in order to close off the last line of defence of determinism, which we found compelled to retreat from action-event compatibilism to mind–body interactionism, and then finally to identity theory. The last position is the most plausible form of determinism but we have seen that, under sufficient probing, it too lapses into inconsistency. The case would seem to be closed in favour of a libertarian conception of man as a free agent whose actions and avowals are explainable only by his reasons, purposes and values, rather than by either physical or mental causes. In brief, a human being is a person, not an automaton.

# 6 Person and Self

'... only of a living human being and what resembles (behaves like) a living human being can one say: it has sensations; it sees; is blind; hears; is deaf; is conscious or unconscious' – Wittgenstein, *Philosophical Investigations*

Ascription of psychological predicates involves reference to the beliefs, values and purposes of the agent. Thus psychological knowledge is founded on the agent's avowals, whereby he exercises a power, bestowed on him by his fellow agents who recognise his privileged authority to establish by declaration the significance, for him, of what is happening to him and what he is doing in response. In so avowing, to himself or to others, he declares his reasons in terms of which his actions can be understood and evaluated. He 'explains himself', to himself as well as to others. It follows that, to be a psychological subject, i.e. a rational agent, one must be capable of self-consciousness; one must have a 'self' to explain. What kind of creature is capable of such agency, and what kind of entity is the 'self' he must have and be aware of? We call such an agent a *person*. What then is it to be a person, and what is it to have a self?

Traditionally, the concept of person has been defined either in terms of a collection of mental states (the 'bundle theory' of Hume) or as a substance in which such states 'inhere' (the 'substance theory' of Descartes). As Sidney Shoemaker has shown convincingly in his *Self Knowledge and Self Identity*[1] both views lead to incoherence, for the substance theory cannot provide criteria for the identification of different manifestations of the same person and the bundle theory cannot provide criteria for distinguishing different persons. Shoemaker's lucid account is somewhat marred by his use of 'person' and 'self' interchangeably, a use which, I shall argue later, is mistaken. But he establishes the important fact that 'it is essential and central to the notion of a person that there be such non-criterial [i.e., authoritative] self-knowledge'.[2] Note that the concept of person includes that of self, from which it follows that the two concepts, while logically related, are not equivalent. But Shoemaker sets us on the right track toward a clearer understanding of these two concepts, and Strawson, as we shall see, guides us still further, if not quite all the way.

In his chapter on Persons, in *Individuals*,[3] Strawson argues that persons are a basic type of individuals, distinct from bodies but more complex, in that persons *have* bodies. Despite the fact that the idea of a disembodied person is incoherent, Strawson suggests, 'person' cannot be defined as a union of a mind with a body, since the possession of mental properties as well as physical properties presupposes that the owner is a person, and cannot therefore serve as an analysis of person into these two features. The concept of person, Strawson maintains, is 'logically primitive', i.e. unanalysable into necessary and sufficient conditions. Most philosophers have assumed that any creature observed to have psychological states is thereby empirically classifiable as a person, in the way any organism that synthesises chlorophyll can be classified as a green plant. But Strawson's subtle point is that the criteria of any particular psychological state or property are indistinguishable from criteria of physical properties unless the subject has *already* been identified as a person.

Thus the difference between a machine that simulates mental skills and a human being that really has them is to be found, not in the observable properties of each, but in the semantical inappropriateness of psychological predicates to machines, and their appropriateness to human beings, insofar as the latter, and not the former, are recognised as persons *independently* of their observable movements. Indeed a movement of an object can be seen either as a mere movement or as an action, depending on whether or not we already assume the object to be a person. If the object makes sounds that resemble speech, we interpret such sounds as speech only if we already assume the object to be a person. Thus no matter how well Turing's machine simulates human speech responses to our questions, we need not regard it as a person capable of psychological states since we know it to be a machine. But if 'person' cannot be defined, psychological predicates ('P-predicates') can be, as predicates that are both self-ascribable without observation and other-ascribable on the basis of 'logically adequate behavioural criteria'.[4]

Let us consider in detail the relation between the concept of a person and the criteria of psychological predicates, by examining the arguments of A. J. Ayer in defence of the traditional view that to be a person is either to *have* (substance theory) or to *be* (bundle theory) a collection of P-predicates. On Ayer's view, the mental properties of others are known only by analogy between their behaviour and one's own behaviour whose mental antecedents are known to oneself by introspection. Consequently we can always, in principle, be mistaken in ascribing P-predicates to others and we can therefore also be mistaken in inferring that another creature is a person equipped with a *bona fide* mind. The problem of whether there are other minds besides our own is therefore, for Ayer, insoluble. It will be useful for our general purpose to take a careful look at Ayer's reasoning against

Strawson's claims that (1) person status is logically prior to assigning P-predicates and (2) on the assumption that a certain creature is a person, we can ascribe P-predicates to him on the basis of logically adequate behavioural criteria, and he can ascribe them to himself without criteria. For if Ayer is right, then a person can be defined as a creature who has psychological properties or mental states, but, on the other hand, we can never know for sure if any creature other than ourselves does, in fact, have such properties. I want to argue here, in defence of Strawson, that Ayer is mistaken on both counts, that is, the concept of a person is *not* definable in terms of the manifestation of psychological properties, for these presuppose person-status; but on the other hand any given psychological property can, under certain conditions, be ascribed with certainty to a subject *already* granted the status of a person. In brief, Ayer's scepticism is directed toward the wrong target: it is person status that is not provable, rather than the possession by a person of any particular psychological property. After meeting Ayer's criticism of Strawson, I shall explain the logical role in language of the concept of a person and its relation to the concept of self.

P-PREDICATES

In his essay, 'The Concept of a Person', Ayer argues that Strawson's notion of logically adequate behavioural criteria of P-predicates is incoherent, offering two main arguments to this effect, a dilemma and a *reductio ad absurdum*. The dilemma is this: either the behavioral criteria of P-predicates are linked to them by definitions or they are not logically adequate. If the former, then reductionism is right. If the latter, then introspectionism is right. In either case, Strawson must be wrong.[5]

Ayer's second argument involves an imaginary experiment in which a child is brought up among robots and taught psychological language by a tape-recorded voice that describes the robots as if they were persons, attributing the same psychological states to both robot and child when they make similar sounds and movements. The child then would learn to apply P-predicates to himself correctly and to the robots mistakenly, from which it follows that behavioural criteria of such predicates cannot be logically adequate, i.e. they cannot guarantee correct application.

I shall try to show that both of Ayer's arguments are unsound, the first because it oversimplifies the notions of behaviour and logical adequacy, the second because it conflates two problems that should be kept separate. I shall begin with the second argument, because the plausibility of the first depends upon the equivocation involved in the second.

## The Case of the Clever Robots

Ayer's description of his imaginary experiment in child rearing betrays a simplistic identification of human behaviour with physical movements, that, if unchallenged, would justify the reductionism he wants to avoid. The child in his *Gedankenexperiment* is taught the use of psychological concepts by a recorded voice that attributes P-states to the robots when they make the appropriate gestures and sounds. But it is essential to Strawson's account of P-predicates that mere physical movements cannot be identified with human actions. Strawson says:

> ... we understand ... we interpret (bodily movements) only by see-
> ing them as elements in just such plans or schemes of action as those
> of which we know the present course and future development with-
> out observation of the relevant movements. But this is to say that we
> see such movements as actions, that we interpret them in terms of
> intention. ... It is to say that we see others as self-ascribers, not on
> the basis of observation, of what we ascribe to them on this basis.[6]

Now if, to interpret physical movements as criteria of P-states of a person, one must 'see' the initiator of these movements as a self-ascriber, then Ayer's robots cannot be mistaken by the child for real persons, because the tape-recorded voice cannot get him to see the robots as *self-ascribers*. Only the robots could accomplish that deception by simulating the behaviour of self-ascribers, that is, by talking about themselves.

So the robots would have to teach the child psychological language by ascribing P-predicates to themselves as they perform appropriate actions, e.g. saying 'I am angry at you, I intend to spank you', and then spanking the child, just like real parents in the good old days. If the tape-recorded voice alone were to perform this pedagogical task, the child would soon come to regard the voice as the voice of a person (and correctly so) and the robots as merely the distant body organs of that same person, and he would be as close to the truth of the matter as the oddities of his eerie world permit. No doubt his idea of *another* person would differ from ours. He would think the world contains two persons: one (himself) with a head, two arms, a torso, and two legs connected vertically in that order; and the other a set of spatially separated metallic limbs controlled by a centrally located metallic head (the tape recorder). How easy or hard it would be for this poor child to develop filial feelings toward his mechanical 'daddy' (or 'mummy'?) is a matter of speculation. Recent experiments in which rhesus monkeys were nourished by robots indicated that simian babies can develop as strong attachments to dummies as to mummies. But we may doubt whether human children can be satisfied by milk without human kindness. In any case, the child's concept of a person would *not* be erroneous, for the recorded voice *is* the voice of a person. At worst, only his knowledge of biology would suffer.

But suppose Ayer were to amplify his imaginary experiment to meet this objection by postulating that a gifted engineer builds into the robots mechanisms that produce appropriate sounds on appropriate occasions so as to simulate rational and emotional discourse. Suppose then that the robots are programmed to say 'I am angry' when the child strikes them and then to spank the child; to say 'I love you' when the child kisses them and then to kiss the child and, in general, to make just the sounds that we ordinarily interpret as self-ascriptions of P-predicates, and to perform just the movements that we ordinarily interpret as motivated actions. Would the child then learn to ascribe P-states mistakenly to the robots while ascribing them correctly to himself?

This amplified hypothesis must be looked upon with suspicion because it cannot even be stated without begging the crucial question as to whether genuine discourse and emotional behaviour *can* be mechanically simulated to perfection, which is precisely the issue in contention between Ayer and Strawson. To begin by assuming that Strawson is wrong will not advance our understanding of the problem.

But whether Ayer's argument is question-begging is not the most important issue at stake. It is of more interest to decide whether his hypothesis, in the revised form, is a coherent one. Is it theoretically possible for machines to simulate human discourse and behaviour with sufficient accuracy to provide a child with adequate and yet misleading paradigms of psychological states? Put in this way, the question smells of paradox. How can paradigms be both adequate *and* misleading? We are entitled to suspect that the hypothesis is, in fact, incoherent. Our problem will be to pinpoint where and how it goes wrong.

Now the issue as to whether robots can effectively simulate human behaviour may be understood in two importantly different ways: (1) as the question how we know a creature, X, is a person and (2) *assuming* X to be a person, how we know from his behaviour that he is in a specific P-state.[7] Ayer's preoccupation with the problem of other minds led him to interpret Strawson as if Strawson were offering an answer to the first question whereas, if I understand him, Strawson was only concerned with the second.[8] In clarifying the first problem we shall be able to see what is wrong with Ayer's *Gedankenexperiment* and in clarifying the second we shall find a way out of his logical dilemma.

The first problem, how we know whether a creature is a person or a robot (or whether robots can perfectly simulate persons), may be seen in a new light by reversing Ayer's experiment of the child and the robots, and considering how we, who were presumably correctly trained in the use of psychological language, would decide if a creature

who lands in a spaceship from Mars is a person or just a robot. Let us
set aside important, but for our purpose, distracting matters of morpho-
logy and biochemistry by assuming that our Martian looks enough
like a human and enough unlike one so that its appearance provides no
decisive clue, and that its substance is somewhat like but also somewhat
unlike animal tissue so that we cannot be sure if it was manufactured
or just grew. If we are to have criteria of its status as person or robot,
they will have to be behavioural. Now suppose this creature moves and
sounds very much like us, it does things that strikingly resemble walk-
ing, talking, responding to our speech and gestures, perhaps not exactly
like anyone of us, but then neither are we exactly like each other.
Would we automatically admit this creature into the Kantian society
of rational beings? No doubt, some of us would; but others, more
stubbornly sceptical, would suspect it to be a product of Martian
engineering, able to simulate psychologically motivated behaviour
although cold and empty 'inside', lacking the 'internal' states of feeling and emotion that real persons have. Would there be any rational
ground for denying such sceptics a logical right to be sceptical? I can
think of no logical or semantical rule they might be accused of vio-
lating. In other words, we simply do not have established criteria for
deciding whether *creatures other than human beings* are to be considered as persons subject to psychological description.

We are logically entitled to take any common properties of our
human paradigms as criteria for applying the concept of a person to
troublesome cases, but we are equally entitled to refuse the concept
further application. A sensible and kindly man will treat a creature as
a person if that creature exhibits many behavioural features in common
with humans, so a sensible and kindly man will be considerate to dogs
and Martian strangers. But Descartes was within his semantical rights
in regarding animals as automata, and we would have the same right
to suspect our Martian to be a robot. So Ayer is right that there are no
generally established logically adequate behavioural criteria of being a
person, but wrong in thinking that we *need* criteria. The problem of
other minds is indeed insoluble (except by arbitrary decision) *when it is
a problem*. But it *is* a problem only in very odd circumstances.[9]

Having separated the problem of other minds from that of criteria
of specific P-predicates, and having granted Ayer the inconclusiveness
of the former with respect to cases other than human beings, we can
now return to the lonely child among robot companions and see more
clearly what is wrong with Ayer's description of the situation. For we
can now distinguish two possible cases: either (1) Ayer's robots are so
clever that even we, who know the correct use of P-predicates, cannot
be sure whether they are persons or robots, or (2) they are clumsy
enough to provide adequate grounds for identifying them as robots.

In the first case, the child would *not* be falsely or incorrectly ascribing

P-predicates to the so-called 'robots', for if they are so like us that we cannot distinguish them from our fellowmen, we have only Ayer's word for it that they are robots and, *ex hypothesi*, we have no reason to *take* his word for it. Indeed, to take his word for it is to beg the issue at stake by assuming that a person must have private mental states that can remain unknown to others. It is to assume that being a person is a matter of internally observable events. But since person-status is *presupposed* by the ascriptions of any P-predicates, the concept of a person must have a different linguistic function; it is not the name of a set of internal happenings, but rather a warrant for ascribing human characteristics (and especially P-predicates) to a subject so identified.

In the second case, where there are clear behavioural grounds for identifying the child's companions as robots, the child who is taught to describe their sounds and movements in words that *we* use to describe persons would not, as Ayer claims, be falsely ascribing psychological predicates to robots. He simply would not have acquired a vocabulary of genuinely *psychological* predicates. His word 'person' would mean any creature that makes sounds and motions common to him and his robots; and his predicates, 'angry', 'sad', and the like, would designate for him, not psychological states, but behavioural dispositions of which robots are as capable as people. Instead of having learned to apply psychological concepts to himself truly and to the robots falsely, as Ayer envisions the matter, the child would simply have learned a neutral language of the kind now popular among experimental psychologists and engineers.

Thus the success of Ayer's *Gedankenexperiment* rests on an equivocation between case (1) where robots are indistinguishable from persons and thus robots only by Ayer's arbitrary nomenclature and case (2) where the robots are plain robots. Once we note the incompatibility of the two cases, Ayer's counter example to Strawson's thesis collapses, since it can be seen to depend upon the inconsistent hypothesis that both cases hold simultaneously.

## The Dilemma and the Way Out

Having rid ourselves of the red herring problem of how we know that a creature is a person, we can turn to the more genuine Strawsonian problem of how, assuming $x$ to be a person, we can know by observation and with logical certainty what psychological state $x$ is in. Strawson claims that it is of the essence of a P-predicate that it can be ascribed to others on the basis of logically adequate behavioural criteria. We can now take up Ayer's first argument against Strawson, namely, the dilemma that if behavioural criteria entail P-states then P-states are nothing but behavioural tendencies and reductionism is right, while if the criteria merely provide inductive evidence for P-states, then they are not logically adequate and introspectionism is right. According to

Ayer, there is no third possibility in sight. In what follows I shall attempt to sketch out just such a third possibility.

Ayer seems to think of the relation between a state s and its criterion C as either the law-like but contingent relation between two regularly associated facts (e.g. fever and micro-organic infection), or as the analytic relation between a concept and its defining properties (e.g. being a bachelor and being unmarried). Both models are too simplistic to do justice to the linguistic role of a criterion.

The first step in finding a more adequate explication of the relation between criterion and state is to distinguish between the unrestricted logical implication that holds between a term and any part of its definition (as in bachelor–unmarried) and the contextually limited implication that holds only under standard conditions between a dispositional concept and its operational criteria. This relation was made formally precise by Rudolf Carnap in 'Testability and Meaning'.[10] Carnap suggested that dispositional predicates like 'soluble in water' require a special and incomplete mode of definition which he called, 'reduction sentences'. A reduction sentence contains a major conditional clause that specifies the standard test conditions (e.g. the condition that $x$ be placed in water) for the implication asserted in the consequent clause between the disposition (soluble) and its criterion (dissolves). Formally,

$$(x)[Q_1(x) \supset (Q_2(x) \supset Q_3(x))]$$

where '$Q_1$' designates the test condition of being placed in water, '$Q_2$' designates the criterion, dissolves, and '$Q_3$' the dispositional property of being soluble in water. Gilbert Ryle, in accounting for psychological states as behavioural dispositions, seems to have been guided by a similar model.[11] But the model is still too simple. For the open texture of psychological predicates like 'angry' prevents us from listing any observable conditions under which '$x$ is angry' entails or is entailed by one or more observable responses such as '$x$ shouts' or '$x$ attempts to strike $y$', etc. To specify such standard conditions we would need invariant laws of psychology and it is no secret that we have no such laws.

But Carnap's notion of dispositional implication at least sets us on the right track in exhibiting contextual limitations on the scope of the implication. Such limitations are bound to be more complex for P-predicates than for physical properties for two reasons: (1) the lack of invariant laws and (2) a factor which, I believe, explains why there cannot be invariant laws of psychology, namely, the semi-evaluative function of P-predicates.

Take, as a test case, the predicate, 'angry at $y$'. We have already noted the folly of assuming that there is any single response such as $x$ striking $y$, or any finite disjunctive set of responses (such as $x$ striking or shouting at or insulting or shooting or . . . *y*) entailing or entailed by '*x* is angry at *y*'. It is conceivable that *x* might be angry at *y* and do none of these things and that *x* might do any of these things without being angry. The type of response that we may reasonably interpret as anger depends on our evaluation of the circumstances. Suppose that *x* is the clandestine mistress of a public official, *y*, and that *y* has cast her off. On encountering *y* in a public place, *x* embraces and kisses him in order to embarrass him. Seen in this light, kissing qualifies as a normal anger response because of the special circumstances. On the other hand, suppose *x* is an employee of *y*, *y* fires *x*, and *x* kisses him. The kiss in this case is surely not a normal expression of anger. We would have to inquire further to find out just what psychic state it manifests. So the relation between P-predicates and their criteria is limited by two general conditions: (1) that the eliciting circumstances be of a kind appropriate to the P-state in question and (2) that the state be manifested by normal responses, i.e. responses appropriate to the eliciting circumstances. In the case of anger, we indicate the relevant circumstances by saying that the agent was provoked, and we signify the appropriateness of the response by saying that he responded in a normal way, or was in a normal state of mind.

Applying these considerations to the problem of formulating logically sufficient criteria for P-predicates like anger, we need a formula like a Carnapian reduction sentence, but more suitable to the open texture and evaluative force of psychological concepts. Anthony Kenny's illuminating analysis of the criteria of emotions helps make clear what must go into such a formula. Kenny identifies three kinds of criteria of emotions, all of which apply in simple, paradigm cases, but any of which may be absent in special cases: (1) provocation, (2) physiological symptoms, and (3) behavioural responses.[12] Kenny points out that while none of these is a necessary condition for the correct ascription of an emotion, their conjunction is a sufficient condition. Following this lead, we might construct a reduction formula or meaning postulate for '*x* is angry at *y*' by specifying the general restriction of P-predicates to persons, and the three suggested behavioural criteria, as follows: If *x* and *y* are persons and *y* provokes (does something bad to) *x*, then, if *x* is agitated (flushes, pales, clenches his teeth, perspires, etc.) and *x* does or tries to do something appropriately bad to *y* (retaliates), then *x* is (necessarily) angry at *y*. Formally,

$$\text{Necessarily: } (x)(y)\{(Px\&Py\&P^r yx) \supset [(Sx\&Rxy) \supset Axy]\}$$

In criticism of this formula it might be argued that, while the formula gives conditions that are *empirically* sufficient for (i.e. have a high correlation with) the state of anger, it does not provide *logically* sufficient conditions, because we can conceive of cases where all the antecedents of the formula hold and the consequent does not. Such counter-instances, it will be conceded, are fairly rare, for if they were frequent, it is hard to see how anyone could learn to identify psychological states at all. Nonetheless, the argument will go, no finite list of conditions can logically rule out all possible exceptions, and therefore no finite list can provide logically adequate criteria.

Now it seems to me that, plausible as this objection may sound, it *must* be wrong, because we not only learn to apply P-predicates to simple cases where all the above criteria work, but we also learn how to identify the exceptional cases where our criteria break down. This second step makes all the difference between a naïve and a sophisticated understanding of psychology. Now if we can learn how and when to spot exceptions, then the exceptions themselves must come under general rules, and we can build these rules into our formula. Let us try to classify the *types* of possible exceptions, and perhaps we will find either that our formula has already excluded them, or that a slight modification of the formula will serve that purpose. For the ascription of emotions such as anger, the exceptions to our criteria can, I think, be subsumed under three general types as follows: (1) cases where alternate emotions may explain the observed behaviour; (2) cases where purely rational considerations, i.e. practical or moral reasons rather than emotional states, may explain the observed behaviour, and (3) cases where the emotion is simulated rather than genuine. Let us then consider whether our formula has already ruled out these cases and, if not, whether it can be adequately modified.

*Type 1* (alternate emotions): $x$ may show agitation and respond aggressively, yet be motivated by some state other than anger, for example, fear. In such a case, the factor that distinguishes fear from anger (or from a mixture of both) may be found in subsequent responses of the agent. If $x$ strikes $y$ in fear rather than in anger, he will desist when he finds that $y$ is stronger than he or when the danger $y$ presents to him is removed. But if he is acting in anger, he will continue to react beyond the needs of self-defence and even contrary to such needs.

*Type 2* (non-emotional reasons): $x$ may respond aggressively to $y$ for reasons that are, in themselves, non-emotional in either of two ways – $x$ may be acting to achieve some practical goal such as the deterrence of further aggression by $y$, or for the sake of some moral principle such as professional duty or social justice. But these cases are already ruled out in our formula by the condition of symptomatic agitation. It may be argued that all responses to provocation, no matter how rational their justification, are attended by some degree of agitation. But if so, then all such responses are, to some degree, emotional, and there can be no counter-instances of this type to our formula, which purports to give *sufficient*, but not necessary conditions for ascribing anger. There is no need to exclude the possibility that an angry person has a good practical or moral reason for retaliating against those who provoke him.

*Type 3* (simulated emotion): What of those cases where $x$ is merely simulating anger, like the politician whose constituents expect a proper fury at high taxes, communist victories, or crime in the streets, or the Method actor who convinces himself in order to convince his audience? This kind of exception literally proves our rule, for how could it be possible to simulate a state if there were no adequate criteria to take advantage of? What could one *do* to simulate anger, if the state of anger were logically independent of behaviour? The very possibility of pretence entails, not the logical insufficiency of criteria of the state that is simulated, but rather the possibility of our being mistaken as to whether the criteria are in fact satisfied. A counterfeit bill is not one that satisfies the criteria of a bank note yet somehow fails to be one, but one that superficially appears to satisfy, yet on closer inspection can be seen not to satisfy the appropriate criteria. Similarly if $x$ is simulating anger, then he is not really agitated or not really trying to injure $y$, and sufficiently close inspection should reveal that one or both of these criteria are not in fact satisfied.

I can imagine no other types of possible exceptions, real or apparent. This, of course, is not to say that no other exceptions can be found. Still less can I claim to have proven that *all* P-predicates have logically adequate behavioural criteria, even if my formula were conceded to work for the particular predicate 'angry at'. But I doubt if Strawson meant to claim that *all* P-predicates have adequate criteria. Predicates signifying long-term states or traits, e.g. 'loves', 'is honest', 'is ambitious', probably do not have adequate criteria for the reason that no time limits can be agreed upon for their correct ascription. A man may act like a lover, may behave impeccably, or may pursue public honours for a time and then stop. Are we to say that he loved but no longer loves, that he was honest for a while but became corrupt, that he had, but then lost, ambition or should we say that he was not really in love, not really honest, nor really ambitious? There simply are no precise rules governing such a decision. But as I understand Strawson, he claims only that those P-predicates that can be ascribed to oneself without observation (and thus with absolute authority) must also be ascribable to others on the basis of logically adequate behavioural criteria. Now long-term attitudes or traits can no more be ascribed to oneself with non-observational authority than they can be ascribed to others with empirical certainty.

At the other end of the psychological spectrum, predicates that signify very transient states, e.g. feelings, sensations and moods, are particularly easy to ascribe by means of behavioural criteria. A groan subsequent to an injury, a radiant smile after winning a contest are (setting aside the special problem of simulation with which we have already dealt) logically sufficient criteria of pain and pleasure. My reason for choosing the predicate, 'angry at', as a test of Strawson's thesis was that it falls just about halfway between the easy short-term cases and the impossible long-term cases. I think that Strawson would have to grant that there are no logically adequate behavioural criteria for very general and long-term P-predicates, but the concession would not endanger his thesis. Persistent attitudes like love and character traits like honesty can be explicated, *à la* Ryle, as tendencies to experience certain short-term states like affection or desire, to perform certain activities like doing favours or telling the truth, and to manifest agitation on appropriate occasions – in brief, they may be explicated as tendencies to definite P-states, rather than as definite P-states in their own right.

It has not been my intention to attempt the impossible task of proving that *all* P-predicates have logically adequate behavioural criteria, nor even of proving this for the single predicate, anger. I have tried only to sketch out the schematic form in which adequate criteria could be articulated and to fill out the form plausibly for the predicate, anger, in such a way as to show a possible escape from Ayer's dilemma. I do not pretend to have proven that Strawson *is* right, but only that it is possible that he is right. Nor am I at all confident that Strawson would recognise his baby in all these new clothes.

PERSONAL IDENTITY AND SELF

Having disentangled the question of how we can know that another creature is a person (the problem of 'other minds'), from that of how we can know that a given P-predicate is ascribable to a given person (what psychological state he is in), we can return to the first question and sum up the matter as follows: the observable behaviour of a creature provides us with adequate criteria for ascribing to it a certain psychological state if and only if we already regard that creature as a person to whom it makes *sense* to ascribe *any* P-predicates. As for how we know that *x* is a person, the answer suggested was that we assume without criteria that all humans are persons. As for non-humans, if their behaviour is strikingly like ours, we may reasonably include them in our club, or we may refuse to do so. Logic and language alone cannot decide the matter for us. For even the apparent self-ascriptions (avowals) of robots can, without semantical error, be classified as simulated, rather than real self-ascriptions, and as simulated rather than real speech. If one insists that, whatever apparent self-ascriptions a creature makes, and however rationally governed its 'actions' seem, the creature's sounds and movements are mere sounds and movements resulting from antecedent physical causes, there are no grounds on which we can prove him wrong.

It would appear that person status resembles the supervenient character of evaluative predicates like 'good', pointed out by Hare in *The Language of Morals*, and by Gallie in 'Essentially Contested Concepts'.[13] While observed behaviour provides us with grounds for assigning person status, these grounds are never logically conclusive; they do not entail such status. A decision must be made as to whether or not to *take* such grounds as adequate. Compare concepts of social roles such as doctor, leader, friend. Person is the genus of which these are species.

As already noted, we do not need empirical grounds for recognising our fellow human beings as persons; rather, we generally follow the rule that any creature born of woman is *prima facie* entitled to person status. I say we *generally* follow this rule, because we do not always do so. Very small children, mentally defective humans, and household pets are granted only semi-person status; the avowals of the first two groups are not taken as authoritative while domestic pets are incapable of avowals. In all three cases, the subjects are granted only some of the rights of personhood but not all and, which perhaps amounts to the same thing, a much smaller segment of their behaviour is explained psychologically rather than causally.

Many people refuse to grant full person-status even to some of their rational and adult fellowmen. Racism, ethnocentrism, chauvinistic nationalism and extreme self or family-centredness are attitudes expressive of the conviction that members of another race, ethnic group, or nation, or humans outside one's family, or even any human other than oneself, deserve only some rights (perhaps none) but not all; that their needs and interests need not be considered, and that we need not bother to evaluate their conduct, but need only train and condition them, like domestic animals. Such attitudes cannot be sustained without considerable self-deception and are therefore morally pathological. Nevertheless, as Sartre eloquently describes them in his *Portrait of the Anti-semite*, such attitudes are *menschlich, allzumenschlich*, demonstrating that, even with respect to human beings, the status of person can be problematic.

But is not 'person' merely a synonym for 'normal and mature human being'? When a sign declares 'There is room for twenty persons in this elevator', do we understand this to mean that there is room for twenty human beings? Clearly not. The substitutability in this context of one concept for another is coincidental and does not argue for semantical equivalence. A chimpanzee would count as an occupant of the elevator, but not as a person. And an infant in its mother's arms would count as a person, but not as an occupant.

Secondly, and more important, is the difference in *use* between 'person' and 'human being'. The latter term is semi-biological, semi-normative, while the former is purely normative.[14] 'Human' spans the fact–value gap through its dual use, being limited in reference to *homo sapiens* at the same time that it conveys more than biological taxonomy, as in 'He's only human', 'It's inhuman to behave that way'. 'Person', on the other hand, is open-ended in reference. It is possible to conceive of persons other than human beings, such as gods, angels, Martians, etc. The reason for this open-endedness is that 'person' indicates a subject of psychological and moral predicates, independently of biological classification.

The concept of a person is a public, social concept, while that of self is intimate and private. Locke seems to have had this consideration in mind when he defined a person as a creature with human traits, and the self (which he wisely distinguished from the soul, although he was wrong to distinguish soul from person) as the continuity of one's memories. Shoemaker, criticising Locke, cites Reid and Butler in arguing that memory cannot be the criterion of personal identity, first, because identity preserves through loss of memory, and second, because in order to know that memories are one's *own*, one must have an independent way of identifying oneself. But Shoemaker wrongly treats personal and self-identity as synonymous.[15] The very phrase, 'self-identity' sounds wrong. With whom else could one be identical, if not oneself? This fact is so trivial that the relation of identity seem vacuous here.

Consider the grammatical uses of 'person' and 'self'. We use 'person' to identify others, not ourselves (except insofar as we are not sure who we are *for others*, our public identity, name, family, occupation, etc.). We count persons, describe them and identify them. One cannot do any of these things with selves. Grammatically, the term 'self' is purely reflexive in use, which is why there need be no procedures or criteria of self-identification. This may account for the philosophical muddles about the criteria of personal identity. As Shoemaker rightly notes, the identification of other persons requires criteria, while self-identification does not. But Shoemaker draws a misleading conclusion from this *aperçu*. He concludes that one knows one's own *personal identity* without criteria, and this, we have already seen, is not the case. I know that I am Raziel Abelson by just the same methods that others know who I am (birth certificate, etc.). As for my *self*, it makes no sense to say that I know I am myself, on the Wittgensteinian ground of vacuous contrast, that I cannot fail to know this trivial grammatical fact if I know how to use the reflexive personal pronoun, 'myself'. The only knowledge here involved is that of English grammar.

But often the expression 'self' is used in a more interesting way, both in everyday discourse and in philosophical discussions. When a person announces, 'I'm not myself today', or criticises an actor's performance as 'too self-conscious', or when philosophers debate the merits of 'substance' vs 'bundle' theories of self, or when psychologists write of the development in the child of a sense of self, they surely mean by 'self' more than mere grammatical first-person reflexivity of reference. What more could they mean?

Perhaps the best way to get at the answer to this question is by considering what such people are trying to *exclude* when they speak of the 'self'. We might ask with what the self is being contrasted, if it is not simply identical with the speaker. In speaking of self in any of the above ways, one is surely not merely picking out one person from among others, for if so, then 'self' would have only the trivial grammatical reflexive use we have already discarded. And since persons *have* selves, in the more interesting philosophical sense of 'self', then the self must be some part or aspect of the person speaking (or spoken of) which may be distinguished from the other, somehow less essential parts or aspects of that person. Well then, just which parts or aspects of a person are *not* to be included in this meaning of 'self'?

One might be tempted to begin the list of what is not the self by excluding all bodily parts and features, as traditional dualism has done, thus confining the self to the mind, or perhaps some peculiarly central 'part' of the mind, such as emotion, will or reason. There are reasons for proceeding in this way, but there are better reasons for not doing so. We know ourselves in a more direct and authoritative way than we know others, as we saw in Chapter 2. Now this would *appear* not to be true of our bodily parts and aspects. The agnosomiac mistakenly believes that he still has his amputated limb. One may think one is thin when in fact one is rather pudgy, that he is graceful when in fact he is clumsy. Descartes appealed to these considerations in concluding that he is not his body at all.

But is all knowledge of our bodily parts and features of this fallible character? On reflection it is clear that we have non-observational and thus authoritative knowledge of our bodily features and actions as well as of our 'mental' experiences. Is hunger not bodily as well as mental, are pain and sensual pleasure not just as physical as they are mental? As for action, I normally know what I am doing without having to observe myself doing it, e.g. signalling for a turn, puzzling over a problem, cleaning my room, etc. Aside from 'purely mental activities' like dreaming or imagining, doing things involves bodily actions of which we must be authoritatively aware without observation of ourselves. Thus some at least of our bodily actions and features must belong to us as intimately as our thoughts. I mean to claim that this is *normally* the case, not always the case. I may mistakenly believe I am filling a cup with water when in fact I am spilling the water on someone's lap, and only observation (or my victim's curses) can set me straight. Where the concept of what I am doing essentially involves reference to matters not entirely within my control, I cannot know what I am doing in the authoritative sense indicated. I cannot even know for sure that I am pouring water, since the pitcher may contain, say, alcohol, judging from my victim's angry protests. But if I confine my description to what *is* entirely within my control, e.g. 'I am *trying* to pour water into a cup', then, setting aside abnormal cases of self-deception (to be considered later on), I cannot be mistaken.

I have been considering only one's *use* of one's body as central to himself. What of the *parts* of his body – can one not be mistaken about the existence and the features of any part of his body, unlike his states of mind? Shoemaker and Penelhum have shown that there is a conceptual relation rather than a contingent-empirical one between perceptual and memory experiences and the parts of one's body, e.g. between seeing and having eyes directed toward a point of space, although this conceptual relation is more complex than simple entailment. If these arguments are sound, then in order to know that I am perceiving or remembering something, I must also know that I have the bodily apparatus in working condition to perceive or to have (in the case of remembering) previously experienced it. I do not mean to suggest that perceptual and memory reports are infallible (cf. Chapter 2), but only that we normally know that we are perceiving something without observing ourselves perceiving it, or that we are remembering something without observational evidence that it was indeed we who experienced it, and that it follows from these facts that we must also know that we have the bodily equipment in working order to do so without observing our bodies and how they are functioning.

To return to what is involved in our concept of self. In one way, 'self' means more than one's own mind and body, in another way, less. The meaning of 'self' may be approached by considering the various degrees of intimacy implied by the possessive pronoun, 'my'. I may speak of 'my money', 'my land', 'my house', 'my book', 'my child', 'my arm', 'my body', 'my mind', and finally, 'myself'. The differences of degree of intimacy may be recognised by considering to what extent the value of '$x$' in the expression 'my $x$' can be separated from me or lost to me without destroying me. Clearly, money is not mine in a very intimate sense, for it can be transferred from me to someone else without affecting either the money or myself. So too for my land, except insofar as I have come to identify myself with it, through the loving care I have given it. But for many landowners, it is possible to transfer ownership of their land without 'loss of self'. The house in which one lives is usually more than just a house; it is a home, and *my* home cannot easily be transferred to another, to become *his* home. Legal transfer is not enough – the house becomes his home only gradually, as he redecorates it, becomes attached to it, and develops a feeling of being at home in it. Similarly, it ceases to be my home in a gradual and inverse way.

What a person creates – his book, his painting, his sculpture, etc. – is still more intimately his own, so that even if legal ownership has been transferred long ago, it remains his work in a sense of ownership that law cannot create or destroy.[16] For this reason, the labour theory of value of Locke and Marx, whereby the product of one's work still belongs to one despite legally-sanctioned formalities of transfer, strikes one as self-evidently true. A society in which one must sell the product of one's creative and loving care is as inimical to self-fulfilment as one in which a woman must sell her body – perhaps even more so, since the prostitute gets her body back, periodically.

One's child is still more intimately connected with oneself, both because the child is the biological continuation of the bodies of the parents and because the child is, to a greater or lesser extent (depending on how much care the parent has invested), the *magnum opus* of the parent. To lose one's child is, for most parents, to lose the best part of themselves – it is like amputation of one's limb, only worse.

To what degree of intimacy are the parts of one's body one's own? Hippies and small children aside, we feel no sense of amputation in having our hair cut, or our beards shaved, or in paring our fingernails. The sense of amputation, or loss of part of oneself, is experienced in two cases: (1) when the injury to one's body radically changes the appearance by which one is identified by others (disfigurement) and (2) when one loses a part of his body that is essential to his most valued activities. Thus it is less a loss to oneself to lose a toe or a lung than to lose an arm or leg.

Is my mind more myself than my body, as Descartes maintained? I think the answer is both yes and no. To a great extent, although not always, radical psychological changes are more destructive of selfhood than are radical physical changes. One reason for this was pointed out by Ryle, namely, that personality traits and intellectual skills are of more *general* use than bodily traits and skills; they can be employed in a wider variety of ways. A man who has lost his fingers can learn to employ prosthetic devices in their place, but if he has lost his retentive capacity he can learn nothing and so can find no substitute. Having a mind is a necessary condition for being able to use one's body effectively, so that to lose some mental faculty is a more serious loss, of a more central part of oneself, than to lose any non-vital bodily part. Nevertheless it was a mistake for Descartes to conclude that one can still exist, still have one's psychic self, without one's body. It seems possible to imagine changing bodies sooner than changing minds, judging from the wide appeal of doctrines of transmigration. But that is only because we tend to imagine a mind as a quasi or ghostly body, moving from one residence to another, and we fail to attend to the sense of 'my' in which one can speak of 'my mind'. It cannot be mine in being housed in my body, if it can change lodging. Then in what sense is my mind *my* mind? For that matter, in what sense is my body *my* body?

The answer to both questions will, I think, give us a further clue to the meaning of 'self'. My body and my mind are mine in the most intimate sense of possession, according to the criterion of intimacy I have suggested: they are inseparable from myself. The destruction of either is the destruction of my self. But this is not true of my personal identity. Others will continue to recognise me as the same person, even if I lose my mind completely, although of course, there will no longer be anyone to recognise if my body is destroyed. Does this entail the reverse of Descartes' claim – namely that the self is the body, rather than the mind? Having a body is a more essential condition for being a person than having a mind (more accurately, *continuing* to have a body is more essential than continuing to have a mind, since if a creature *never had* a mind, he would be at best only a quasi-person) but the relative importance to oneself of one's physical as against one's mental capacities depends on which one *values* more. The less a person cares about his body, the less central to himself are his bodily organs. While hardly anyone has a sense of great loss if he loses his appendix or gall bladder, most of us feel a loss of a part of ourselves if a limb is amputated. But some care less than others. An athlete who loses a leg may well feel totally destroyed, while a painter or a sculptor might endure losing a leg but not an arm. I would guess that a sculptor could sooner bear the loss of his sight than his sense of touch, while it would be the other way around for a painter, and a musician would find least bearable the loss of his hearing.

I am trying to suggest that, to put it with deliberate Sartrian paradox, one's self is what one identifies oneself with, what a person cares most about, the loss of which amounts, for him, to self-destruction, either partial or total. The phenomenon of the feeling of loss of self has been well studied and described by psychotherapists, some of whom find this to be the most common and also the most serious kind of psychopathology. R. D. Laing describes this phenomenon of 'ontological insecurity':

> ... The individual ... many feel more unreal than real; in a literal sense, more dead than alive; precariously differentiated from the rest of the world, so that his identity and autonomy are always in question. He may lack the experience of his own temporal continuity. He may not possess an over-riding sense of personal consistency or cohesiveness. He may feel more insubstantial than substantial, and unable to assume that the stuff he is made of is genuine, good and valuable. And he may feel his self as divorced from his body.[17]

Laing goes on to explain that this sense of instability or loss of self motivates the psychopath to attempt to 'depersonalise' others and himself, to reduce others and himself to mere things so as to escape his sense of insecurity, very much as Sartre describes the anti-semite in his *Portrait* and the self-deceptive person in *Being and Nothingness*.

Like most other writers, Laing tends to conflate the concept of self with that of personal identity, and the sense of loss of one's identity (which has to do with the way one believes that others see him) with that of loss of self which has to do with uncertainty about one's values and consequent dependence on the opinions and attitudes of others. No doubt these two phenomena are closely related.[18] But for our purpose we can set aside problems of personal identity so as to concentrate on what it is to have or to lack a self.

Of course, no one who is able to use the reflexive first person pronoun 'myself' lacks altogether a sense of himself, and to speak of 'losing oneself' and 'finding oneself' is effusively metaphorical. What can be said more literally is that a person can have a more or less rich and ample, or more or less impoverished and narrow self, and one's awareness of being in the latter state provides him with a reason to feel 'ontologically insecure' and to become excessively dependent upon others, a dependence which consists, I would suggest, in substituting one's public identity in place of one's sense of himself, in order to escape awareness of the poverty of the latter. If so, then the tendency to confuse personal identity with self is not only a philosophical error; it is also injurious to effective psychotherapy.

It is natural to identify the self by means of the biological boundaries of the person – whatever is inside one's skin. Various expressions encapsulate this all-too-natural mis-identification, e.g. 'selfish', 'self-centred', 'self-less devotion', and the old paradoxical cliché: 'One must lose oneself in order to find oneself.' This mis-identification of self with biological organism is due to the fact that our biological longevity and health are of great importance to us – we'd be dead without them. But other things are important to us as well, and not infrequently they are even more important. People often sacrifice their health and sometimes their lives for other values they hold even dearer, such as family, political causes, the advance of science, religious freedom – what they believe will benefit some or all of humanity. In Chapter 8 I shall argue that the foundation of morality lies in the capacity of a person to identify himself to some extent with other persons, in recognising their interests as justifying reasons for action, and their rights as equal to his own.

We have seen that there is a trivial, reflexive use of 'self' whereby the self just is the person speaking, as in 'I cut myself', or the person spoken of, as in 'He cut himself'. But this cannot be the same use as when we speak of self-knowledge, self-deception and self-fulfilment. Here the reference of 'self' lies primarily in the future, while in the trivial reflexive use, it is entirely in the present. In the more philosophically interesting use, the self is both more and less than the immediate person, more because it can include other persons (family, nation, even humanity), and less because many of one's personal features may be considered by him as inessential to himself in that he would not feel mutilated by their loss, e.g. hair, paunch, colour of skin or eyes, memories of childhood, etc.

Sartre has suggestively called the self, in this sense, a *project*, to emphasise its futurity of reference and its dependence on one's choices and actions. A person chooses himself, Sartre maintains, in setting himself goals and acting toward them. Clearly, the self, in this sense, is not an object of inspection and description, and to debate whether it does or does not exist is as pointless as to debate whether the future does or does not exist. Sartre asserts that the self 'exists in the mode of the not-yet', a deliberately paradoxical way of saying that it does not yet exist while also indicating that we have reason to act as if it already exists. This paradox, we shall see, lies at the heart of the phenomenon of self-deception.

Since the interesting philosophical use of 'self' is so paradoxical, denoting an ideal to be realised which we are tempted to treat as a real entity, could we not avoid the logical difficulties by dispensing with this problematic use of 'self' and confining our language to the trivial reflexive use? The reason why that would be unwise is the reason why the philosophical use is so interesting, namely, that without the paradoxical features of concepts like self-knowledge, self-deception, and self-fulfilment, psychological discourse would be so impoverished that it could be dispensed with in favour of behaviouristic jargon. We saw in Chapter 2 that the public incorrigibility of avowals could not be reconciled with behavioural criteria of psychological predicates without the mediating services of the concept of self-deception, whose function is to explain how, for example, one can behave angrily while sincerely avowing that one is not angry. In the following chapter, I shall investigate the paradoxes of self-deception, in order to relieve them of the appearance of contradiction, and in Chapter 8 I shall attempt a similar clarification of the concepts of self-knowledge and self-fulfilment.

# 7  Self-Deception and *Akrasia*

'But at any rate when you say "I am in pain", you want to draw the attention of others to a particular person – The answer might be: "No I want to draw their attention to *myself*" ' – Wittgenstein, *Philosophical Investigations*

' "I" is not the name of a person, nor "here" of a place' – Ibid.

We have arrived at a notion of the self as the ideal person one wants to become, the incarnation of his prudential and moral values. That one has such an ideal of self follows from the concept of a person. Since being a person entails having authority to avow one's reasons for action, and the exercise of this authority involves appeal to prudential and moral rules in justifying a course of action, it follows that, when our actions are inconsistent with our avowed reasons and intentions, we must attribute them to an agent other than that to which the avowals are attributed, an 'alter-ego' which, if it could be consulted, would give different and more consistent reasons. So arises the notion of an unconscious self as the grammatical object of reflexive description, the person who actually did what I did, but not my 'real self' which disapproves of what was done. A split between the actual and the ideal self is necessitated in order to preserve the authority of avowals. If I cannot avow reasons consistent with my actions, then there must be, within me, some other 'I' that can. In brief, where the authority of self-knowledge seems to break down, it is preserved by distinguishing between two different sources of authority, the actual and the ideal self. When one identifies himself with the former, he is in self-deception. When he identifies himself with the latter, he experiences weakness of will.

## THE PARADOXES OF SELF-DECEPTION

Consider the following situation: A friend of ours, Mr Lovewell, is married to a woman of easy virtue. Everyone knows about her except, apparently, Mr Lovewell. If a friend of his is tactless enough to ask him whether he believes his wife is faithful to him, Mr Lovewell replies, 'Of course I do!' with all the symptoms of sincere and confident belief.

His voice does not tremble, his eyes are steady, his smile is a confident smile. Moreover, he behaves accordingly. He makes no effort to keep his wife under surveillance – if anything, he allows her more freedom than most husbands allow their wives without protest. He is hospitable to her male friends no matter how late at night they drop by. He never shows resentment toward her and never complains about her unexplained absences. So far, we might consider him merely a fatuous cuckold.

But there are other features of Mr Lovewell's behaviour that make us doubt that he *really* believes in his wife's fidelity. We notice that he goes out of his way to avoid conclusive evidence of her amorous affairs. When she flirts with another man at a party, he becomes absorbed in conversation with others. He refuses to listen to gossip about her activities even from trusted friends. He never goes home early from his office without first telephoning his wife, and when he does come home, he does not use his key to open the door, but rings the bell and waits to be admitted.

This is surely an abnormal pattern of behaviour. We have a name for it, 'self-deception', and thereby hangs a tale. Is the term 'self-deception' an explanation of the pathology of Mr Lovewell's behaviour, or is it merely a description that itself requires explanation?

The first part of this chapter will be aimed at showing that the latter is the case, i.e. that the concept of self-deception creates problems that call for further explanation; the second part will deal with explanations that have been proposed, but fail to solve all the problems involved, and the third part will present my own synthesis of the four incomplete theories criticised in the second part.

The concept of self-deception is paradoxical on its face. How could anyone deceive himself? For Iago to deceive Othello about Desdemona, Iago must know the truth while managing to keep Othello in ignorance of the truth. Iago produces in Othello the belief in Desdemona's infidelity but he, Iago, does not share that belief. So deception would seem to be a relation between two persons (or quasi-persons – animals can also be deceived), one who knows the truth and another who is ignorant of it, or one who believes what the other disbelieves. How then can one and the same person know and yet not know, believe and yet disbelieve the same thing at the same time? Let us call this the Epistemic Paradox.

There is a second puzzle, or family of puzzles, which I shall call the Psychological–Ethical Paradoxes. The person in self-deception must be sincere in his profession of his belief. Otherwise he is not *self* deceptive, but a hypocrite trying to deceive others about what he really believes. Yet apparently he must also be insincere, since he employs (like Mr Lovewell) various devices and strategies to conceal the truth, strategies such as avoiding unfavourable evidence and concocting far-fetched *ad hoc* explanations for evidence he fails to avoid so as to render the evidence harmless (e.g. 'Of course my wife was upset when I came home early from the office – she wanted to surprise me with a very special dinner, hamburger and french fried potatoes!').

This paradox of sincere and yet insincere profession of belief engenders another. Self-deception appears to be involuntary and yet also voluntary. The self-deceiver cannot be aware of what he is doing, for otherwise his strategy would have no hope of success, he could not really be deceived. Now if he is unaware of what is happening inside himself, then he is in the grip of forces not under his voluntary control and is therefore to be pitied rather than condemned.

On the other hand, no intelligent strategy can be employed unknowingly and involuntarily. Our very criterion of what is within a person's voluntary control is his ability to adapt his responses to the circumstances so as to ensure success – to vary his responses at will. Self-deception is wilful, that is, it serves the agent's purpose and it involves skilful variation of response. Consequently it is subject to our condemnation as a form of deliberate dishonesty.

We have then two baffling paradoxes – the Epistemic and the Psycho–Ethical. How can we explain them so that their logical sting is removed?

PROPOSED SOLUTIONS

Four approaches have been adopted so far: (1) The multiple-agent model of Freud; (2) The dialectical metaphysics of Sartre; (3) The 'just a metaphor' translational approach; and (4) Fingarette's amputation model, which combines elements of the first three. We shall find them all unsuccessful in resolving the paradoxes.

*Freud's Multiple-Agent Model*
Freud's spectacular system of psycho-dynamical theory may be considered an attempt to explain the process of self-deception which, in his view, is far more common than we think – in fact it pervades all of the nine-tenths of the mental iceberg that lurks below the surface.

The guiding principle of Freud's system is the division of the agent into sub-agents, ego, super-ego and id.[1] The beauty of this model is that it seems to enable us to solve our puzzle easily. In self-deception, one or two of these agencies deceives a third. The id, or the super-ego plus the id, hoodwink the ego. But, as Sartre observed, the price of this easy solution is that the reflexivity of self-deception is lost. No longer does one deceive oneself. Self-deception has been reduced to ordinary deception of others. A second defect, to which Sartre also objects for good reasons, is that the ethical paradox of innocence plus guilt is resolved by denying one side of it. The agent appears as a passive victim of competing forces within his unconscious and is no longer responsible for his actions. But then they are not *his* actions, and the agent has been reduced to a mere battlefield – he is no longer an agent.

## The Dialectical Model of Sartre

Sartre's disappointment with Freud's model tempts him to conclude that the paradoxes of self-deception are unsolvable. Consequently he tries to explain them metaphysically, as due to the dialectical nature of consciousness, which 'is not what it is, and is what it is not'.[2] How can one know the truth and yet remain ignorant, how can he believe yet disbelieve? That's easy. It is just what we always do, because that's exactly what it is to be 'for oneself', that is, to exist in the dialectical manner of the *pour-soi*. Self-deception is thus inescapable.[3] What then about the Psycho-Ethical Paradox, that self-deception is both voluntary and involuntary, thus both culpable and innocent? Here is where Sartre is most unsatisfactory. He denies one side of the paradox – the opposite side from Freud. Self-deception is held to be purely voluntary and therefore inexcusable. But this conclusion is ethically unacceptable. Moreover it is inconsistent with his metaphysics. If self-deception is metaphysically inescapable, then it is not within our voluntary control and we are not morally to blame.

## The Translational Model

A third way of escaping the paradoxes is to argue that the notion of self-deception need not be taken literally. On this view no one *really* deceives himself. When we speak of self-deception, we talk metaphorically. What we literally mean is something else; we mean, for example, that a person's belief is manifestly contrary to the evidence, or that he vacillates between belief and disbelief, or that he fails to take notice of unfavourable facts. As Fingarette has shown in convincing detail, all these attempts to translate self-deception into something else fail to answer the crucial question: Is this 'something else' (e.g. drawing the wrong conclusion, or not noticing unfavourable facts, or vacillating between contrary beliefs) done *knowingly* or *inadvertently*? To do justice to the phenomenon the answer must be 'both', but then we are plunged right back into the paradoxes.

## The Self-Amputation Model of Fingarette

In his illuminating monograph, *Self Deception*, Fingarette proposes that we set aside the 'cognitive model' of belief and disbelief, and employ instead a 'volition-action model' of self-deception, by which I take him to mean that we should consider the Psycho-Ethical Paradox more fundamental than the Epistemic Paradox.[4]

Fingarette's explanation of self-deception is that it is an inability to

'avow one's engagements in the world', due to a painful conflict between one's moral image of himself and the actual pattern of his
conduct. To resolve the conflict while continuing the course of action
on which he is immorally engaged, the self-deceiver denies that it is *his*
engagement. 'That's not the real me', he protests, thereby ostracising
a part of himself by regarding it as an alien force. On this model, self-
deception is accomplished by means of self-amputation.[5]

Fingarette's analysis is an interesting and suggestive synthesis of
Freud's concept of ego-defence with Sartre's notion of the self as a
project. But his rejection of the cognitive model results in failure to
confront and to solve the paradoxes which, as we shall see, return to
haunt us. Moreover, Fingarette commits the error, in common with
both Freud and Sartre, of reducing all cases of self-deception to the
case of moral self-deception motivated by shame. While this may be
the most serious and objectionable kind, it is surely not the only kind.
The woman who refuses to believe the announcement that her husband
was killed in action, the would-be virtuoso who practises the violin at
the expense of more profitable studies, unwilling to admit that he lacks
talent, the acrophobe who strides out to the edge of the diving-board
only to shrink back at the last moment, the religious fanatic who
refuses to consider evidence against the occurrence of miracles, all
these may be criticised for irrationality, but not for refusing to acknowledge their moral responsibilities.

Even with respect to moral self-deception, Fingarette, like Freud
and Sartre, fails to distinguish two very different types of cases: (1)
Cases where the agent excuses himself on the ground that his actions
are not really his own, pleading possession or compulsion, and (2) Cases
of self-deceptive casuistry, where the agent seems sincerely to persuade
himself that he was justified in a course of action that is, to us, manifestly immoral.

But the major defect of Fingarette's analysis is that it falls back into
the paradoxes. For we can ask of the 'inability to spell out one's
engagement': Is it truly an inability, thus involuntary, or is it a refusal,
thus voluntary? Does the agent *really* believe that the engagements in
question are not his own, or does he not believe so, but only pretend
so? Is he somehow prevented by some uncontrollable force from
avowing them, or does he deliberately avoid avowing them? Repeating
Austin's metaphor, we once again find our paradoxes grinning up at us
from the bottom of the beer mug.

A SYNTHESIS

A first step toward a new solution to our paradoxes might be that of
bringing to bear on them the Melden–Danto–R. Taylor distinction

between simple or 'basic' and complex or 'non-basic' actions employed earlier in Chapter 3. The paradoxes remain insoluble so long as we assume that activities like self-scrutiny and self-deception are direct or basic actions. One cannot scrutinise oneself in any direct, simple or basic way because, as Ryle observed, in *The Concept of Mind*, the scrutinising subject cannot at the same time be the object of his scrutiny.[6] Nor can one simply or directly lie to oneself. But if we consider complex activities directed toward future states of oneself, these paradoxes of reflexivity dissolve. One can scrutinise – or at least reflect upon – one's past and one's future self, by reminiscence and prospective reflection, neither of which activities is itself a part of what is being reflected on. And surely one can often bring about a state of oneself different from one's present state, e.g. bringing about the extinction of an undesirable habit by placing oneself in a situation in which it will be impossible to satisfy it ('cold turkey') or signing a contract for an enforced savings plan. In these and myriad ways we overcome our 'weakness of will' by depriving ourselves of any opportunity to 'back-slide'.

Now suppose we consider the process of self-deception as a non-basic or complex activity over time, whereby we bring about a change in ourselves from a state of painful knowledge to one of blissful ignorance, by so arranging circumstances that nothing will remind us of what we wanted to forget, while everything around us will distract us from recalling the painful fact. A man goes abroad for a year 'to forget' the woman who jilted him, a harassed housewife goes to the movies 'to forget her troubles'. In such cases, the Epistemic Paradoxes are resolved by the fact that one does not both know and fail to know, or believe and disbelieve *at the same time*, but believes or knows at one time and does not believe (forgets) at a later time. Similarly, the Psycho-Ethical Paradoxes are relieved, in that the self-deceiver can now be described as *voluntarily* and culpably setting out to become ignorant of a painful fact, but as so arranging matters that his state of ignorance or forgetting is induced in him *non-voluntarily* (and to this extent excusably) by the circumstances he has arranged.

A natural objection to this proposal is that there is a world of difference between the case of the person who consciously and deliberately decides to make himself forget, and the self-deceptive person who not only seems unaware of what he is doing, but would vigorously deny that he is trying to produce or maintain a state of ignorance in himself. As Sartre has observed, the project of self-deception is itself founded in an act of self-deception. This perfectly fair objection points to a distinction between two levels, which I shall call (following Ryle) 'first order' and 'second order' self-deception. The first is the attempt described above as bringing about a change in oneself from a state of painful knowledge to one of painless ignorance (or to sustain the latter against all evidence), while the second is the refusal to acknowledge, to oneself or to others, that one is engaging in the first-order project of self-deception.

But now, of course, we must make non-paradoxical sense of the notion of second-order self-deception. In order to perpetrate *this* hoax, one must both know what one is doing and yet not know it, which seems to land us right back in the outstretched tentacles of our paradoxes. For while the process of first-order self-deception involves only indirectly reflexive action over time, the act of second-order self-deception would seem to involve direct reflexivity of just the kind that engenders the paradoxes.

The sincere refusal to acknowledge what it is that one is doing, which constitutes second-order self-deception, would appear to be a simple or basic action (I include under 'action' omissions as well as commissions). For it is something that we just do, or refrain from doing, without there being anything else to do in order to bring about this failure or refusal to acknowledge what our purpose is. How is this possible?

There are familiar situations in which we do things or refrain from doing things without being aware of what we are doing or refraining from doing. Indeed, in most of our complex activities, there are some basic actions of this sort, such as movements of fingers, hands, feet, head and eyes involved in accomplishing a complex task such as type-writing, playing tennis, driving a car or fighting a battle. Yet it would be wrong to say that we do not know that we are performing these basic actions or to deny that we are performing them voluntarily, e.g. moving a certain finger on a typewriter key, shifting one's feet, stepping on a brake or sighting along a rifle barrel. We are unaware of performing these acts only in the sense that we do not attend to them nor do we later remember them, yet we can still be said to have known what we were doing, since these basic actions have a place in the purposive pattern of our complex activity, and since we vary them intelligently. We could, of course, become aware of them were we to pay attention to every detail of what we are doing (as when we first learn to perform such activities) but we deliberately refrain from attending to them just because, as Ryle noted, that would interfere with their effective performance.

Now I would like to suggest that, unlike first-order self-deception, which is a project carried out over an interval of time with the aid of more basic actions and omissions, second-order self-deception is the basic action of refraining from attending to one's project of first-order self-deception, an act of omission that is continuously sustained throughout the interval of time of the first-order project, until the unpleasant fact at issue is successfully forgotten or buried. In addition to this deliberate absent-mindedness, there is the case of the person who wants to come to believe something that he has reason to know is not the case, such as that he is a talented musician or that his disease is curable, and so to achieve and sustain a state of false but comforting belief. In such cases, the act of omission consists in refraining from attending to the disconfirming evidence. But the objection must now be met that constant avoidance of unpleasant evidence requires intelligent strategy and alertness to danger which indicate that the agent is, after all, quite aware of his first-order project of self-deception.

How, for example, can Mr Lovewell avoid noticing that his wife is flirting with another man unless he is already aware that she is doing precisely that? The answer to this objection is that the avoidance of facts does indeed have a certain comical quality; it is absurd, yet not logically absurd. We avoid noticing, not what we are clearly aware of (on pain of contradiction) but what we merely suspect or dimly sense to be on the periphery of our field of attention – in the wings, so to speak, rather than on stage. Should we suspect that some damaging evidence is is on our right, we may fix our attention on what is happening to our left. Quite possibly, what is on our right is not at all the sinister evidence we fear it to be. But naturally we cannot afford to make sure of what we suspect before we take avoidance action. Thus it is of the very nature of avoidance of knowledge that it is less intelligent and efficient an activity than the pursuit of knowledge, which accounts for the comical quality and peculiar pathos of self-deception, and for our feeling that this project is never completely successful. This consideration also helps explain why self-deceptive people often experience moments of terrifying awareness that drive them to drugs or to psychotherapy.

We are in a better position now to see what is plausible in each of the four theories of self-deception previously considered. The translational account is partly right, partly wrong, because while first-order self-deception is literally an attempt to deceive one's projected or future self, second-order self-deception is not literally deception at all. It is a refusal to take note of unpleasant facts, a refusal that is well described in everyday language as 'not facing things', 'turning one's eyes away', 'wearing blinders', and 'ostrich behaviour'.

Freud's division of the self into separate agencies becomes logically acceptable provided that the agencies are understood as modes of functioning separated in time, for example, if the *id* is identified with the momentary self and the *ego* with the future self.

Sartre's notion of the self as project is of course central to the analysis given here, but we see now that we need not accept his paradoxical conclusion that self-deception is both inescapable and yet culpable, once we distinguish the two modes, one of which (second-order) is voluntary and therefore culpable, while the other (first-order) is not.

Fingarette's self-amputation account of self-deception as 'inability to spell out one's engagements in the world', thus amputating the part of oneself consisting in one's unavowed engagements, can now be seen to hold in one way on one level and differently on the other. First-order self-deception of the projected self-to-be is literally self-deception and it is indeed self-amputating because it divides the immediate self or agent from his project self. To whatever extent this attempt succeeds, we have a non-paradoxical answer to the question whether the self-deceiver is really unable or only unwilling to spell out his engagements. On the first-order level, he is unable to do so insofar as he has succeeded in bringing about the desired state of ignorance. But on the level of second-order self-deception, he is simply unwilling to do so and is therefore culpable, although he may well be excused on grounds of his need to escape unbearable suffering.

We seem now to have defused all our paradoxes. Have we then wrapped up the problem? To claim success would be to commit self-deception in the first degree. Austin's frog is still there at the bottom of the mug. For how can one literally deceive what exists only in the future – a self-to-be that is not there to be deceived? Have we then accomplished nothing? I think not. We have made some progress, but a new start is in order.

A NEW START

*The two concepts of self*
We have seen that the four theories of self-deception considered were all partly right, but not right enough because they did not start from a sufficiently clear notion of self. We had already found in Chapter 6 that 'self' is either trivially reflexive or it signifies an ideal, the person whom the agent projects himself to become. Thus it is logically impossible to deceive oneself. For in the trivial reflexive sense of 'self', deception cannot be reflexive. And in the non-trivial, philosophical sense of 'self' as an ideal or project, there does not yet exist a self to be deceived.

But if self-deception is incapable of literal achievement, it does not follow that the concept is dialectical (i.e. self-contradictory) nor inescapably metaphorical. Self-deception is, in fact, often attempted. It follows only that it can never quite succeed. The agent can only believe that he can succeed by committing, in addition to first- and second-order self-deception, a third-order act of self-deception. A further examination of this terminating act may help us to understand why we so often attempt to accomplish the impossible, and thus to answer the question raised at the end of the previous section.

To believe that one has a self within one's body or within one's mind which he can inspect, argue with, and sometimes outwit, is a metaphysical mistake. It is not, however, an innocent mistake but a deliberate one, as Sartre realised and aptly characterised as *mauvaise foi*. For we have seen that it is logically – indeed, self-evidently – impossible to be a direct object of one's own scrutiny. Why then do people seem to succeed pre-eminently in accomplishing this task which is impossible to accomplish?

I suggest that the 'self' we *can* contemplate is not our trivially reflexive self or actual person, but our projected future and *better* person, the ideal person we would like to be and would like others to take us to be. This philosophical self is not completely imaginary, first, because it is continuous with our past and present self, and secondly, because it contains, at its core, the fundamental and universal human values of moral and prudential rationality, values that we share with our fellowmen and that, together with our animal and cultural needs, constitute our human nature, and make possible a community of persons. Nevertheless, the *projected* self does not exist as a real object of either deception or knowledge.

But why then are we so strongly tempted to believe that our 'true' self *does* exist in this manner, separable from our actual conduct and desires? In providing answers to *this* question the Freudian and Fingarette models have an advantage over the Sartrian and translational models. Sartre puts such belief down to fear of freedom as responsibility. The translational accounts explain this belief as an innocent error, which it is not. Sartre is too severe, the translationalists are too permissive. A still more complex account of the self than that provided so far would seem to be required.

According to Freud, the process of maturation toward rational integration of one's goals involves the formation of an 'ego-ideal' with which one aspires to become identical.[7] Freud exaggerated the degree to which this ego ideal is influenced by parents and social conventions (because of his reliance on a causal model of psychological explanation), although there can be little doubt that such influences play an important role, especially in childhood. But that they cannot play an exclusive, i.e. causally determining role, is evident from the fact that each individual has a system of values and goals uniquely his own; his standards of moral and prudential judgment would not be genuine standards but mere habits were he to apply them in a mechanical Skinnerian fashion. Adapting general rules to new cases and forming new rules is as creative an activity in morals and in practical life as it is in art; indeed it is, as Socrates observed, the highest art – the art of living.

It is essential to moral and intellectual growth that one have an idea of the person one wants to be, and it is a useful and natural device to form an image of that person. From there, it is an easy but dangerous step to treat the person one has imagined as a real person, one with whom I can reason, perhaps defeat in debate, perhaps deceive. Is that person the 'real me' or not? The answer would depend on whether one employs a Platonic or a nominalistic criterion of reality. It is my better self and thus more real if, as Plato maintains, the ideal is more real than what falls short of it. Moreover, it is the person I *want* to be, and surely what I want to be is more intimately myself than what I just happen to be at the moment. Or is it? This is another key ambiguity that generates the volitional paradox of self-deception. Do I really want to be better than I am, or am I deceiving myself in thinking so? There would seem to be no single answer to this question. To the degree to which I make an effort, even if not entirely successful, to change for the better and satisfy the standards suggested by my ego-ideal or projected self, to that degree my wanting to become such a person would seem to be sincere. (Sartre recognises this under the name of *authenticity*, although he denies it in the name of *bonne foi*.)[8]

In any case, we can now see the special merit in the Freud–Fingarette model of self-amputation. Whenever we violate our standards of moral and prudential rationality we sell our birth-right for a mess of porridge; we widen the distance between our projected future self and our actual self and then, in identifying ourselves with both what we are and what we want to be, we experience the disorders of what R. D. Laing has called, 'the divided self'. No wonder then that the self-deceiver is more pitied than condemned.[9]

## Self and Contradiction

In *The Problem of the Self*, Henry W. Johnstone has argued the interesting thesis that the idea of self is a 'locus of contradictions'. Deliberately 'grasping the nettle', as he puts it, he proposes that the very function of the idea of self is to accept rather than to solve various paradoxes of reflexivity, such as self-deception, self-knowledge, self-observation and self-criticism.[10] Johnstone develops analytically the Sartrian view that consciousness is by nature dialectical in the precise sense of engendering logical contradictions. Consciousness, he contends, entails self-consciousness – the awareness that one is conscious; the idea of self is of that which is capable of having irreflexive relations to itself. From this standpoint, self-deception (which Johnstone does not go into specifically) is no longer a unique oddity, but merely a particular species of a general oddity, the contradictory character of mind, which as Sartre puts it, 'is what it is not, and is not what it is'.

Johnstone's analysis seems to me correct and illuminating as far as it goes but it does not go far enough. The phenomena of consciousness are indeed paradoxical, but we cannot let the matter rest there by surrendering the basis of all reasoning, the law of non-contradiction. Paradoxes are challenges demanding investigation, but surely not the last word on the subject. If a concept (self) or a family of concepts (self, consciousness, self-consciousness, etc.) engenders paradoxes, we should be able to find a reason for this which, once articulated clearly, also provides the resolution for the paradoxes. I want to suggest that the reason for these paradoxes of reflexivity can be found in the intentional character of consciousness (see Chapter 1) which makes it possible to avow with authority that one is experiencing reflexively a relation that is irreflexive in nature. The paradoxes of reflexivity therefore stem from a still deeper locus of paradoxes, namely, the problem of inconsistent avowals.

## Inconsistent Avowals

It was argued in Chapter 2 that incorrigibility is an essential feature of avowals which enables them to bring into existence the fundamental data on which psychological explanations rest. In Chapter 6, it was argued in support of Strawson that it is as essential for psychological predicates to have sufficient behavioural criteria as it is for them to be authoritatively self-ascribable. If these claims are accepted, a problem immediately arises: what if the P-predicate ascribed by others to a subject on the basis of sufficient behavioural evidence is incompatible with that which the subject ascribes to himself by his avowal? We seem then to face an insoluble paradox, indeed, a naked self-contradiction, for we must then accept as true the statement that subject S has and yet does not have predicate P. The same predicament is created when the subject S ascribes to himself two incompatible predicates, as when a person says: 'I want to do A and yet I don't want to' or 'I believe it and yet I don't believe it'. If his avowals are taken as authoritative, then we cannot reject them even on the grounds of inconsistency. We can of course ask S: 'Don't you mean that you want or believe in some partial sense or respect, and do not want or believe in some other partial sense or respect?' (e.g. you *would* want to do A if the risk were not so great, or you believe in the sense that you recognise the weight of evidence, but you disbelieve in the sense that you are not willing to act accordingly?). But if the subject rejects these suggestions for relieving the contradiction and insists sincerely that he both wants and does not want in the same respect, or both believes and disbelieves, there is nothing that we can do but accept the paradox as unresolved. However, it does not follow that we must accept psychological reality as self-contradictory. We are still entitled to judge that the situation has not been described with sufficient specificity. The subject's avowals are vague; he is not prepared to specify in more detail, nor can we do so for him. Our respect for his authority of self-knowledge prevents us from amending his assertions, but our respect for the law of non-contradiction requires us to consider his avowals insufficiently specific, as when, lacking the word 'ajar', one asserts that a door is both open and yet not open. Had the subject a more specific description of his state available to him, he would not make inconsistent avowals.

Returning to the problem of conflict between self-ascriptions and other-ascriptions, of which self-deception is the most striking case, here too we may alleviate the strain of contradiction by assuming that some third description, if it were available, would resolve the conflict by specifying the different respects in which each of the two incompatible predicates holds. Not having it at our disposal, we must leave the paradoxes unresolved (we can see the general direction of resolution, but not the details) but we can put our failure down to inadequate specificity of information, rather than to any limitations on the law of non-contradiction.

Thus the inconclusiveness of the type of analysis offered earlier to relieve the paradoxes of self-deception is due to its being formulated independently of the self-knowledge of the subject in question. He alone can relieve the paradoxes completely by specifying the exact respects in which each side of the paradoxes holds in his case. Failing such authoritative specification, we are left with a lingering sense of paradox, but we need not regard this ghostly apparition as the ultimate reality.

The important conclusion to draw, for our purposes, from the inadequacy of any description of self-deception made purely from the standpoint of an observer, is that, far from undermining the authority of self-knowledge, the phenomenon of self-deception presupposes such authority and would not make sense without it, since the full resolution of the paradoxes to which it gives rise when externally described can only be provided by the more specific avowals of the self-deceiver, once he becomes undeceived.

WEAKNESS OF WILL

To be unable to bring ourselves to do what we sincerely want to do, or to be unable to refrain from doing what we do not want to do, a phenomenon that we call 'weakness of will', resembles the paradox of self-deception: sincerely believing what one cannot really believe. Both phenomena seem irresistibly to elicit metaphorical explanations. Just as self-deception elicits the metaphor of a divided self, one part of which deceives the other, weakness of will suggests two agents, one of which overpowers the other. In the effort to translate these metaphors into literal language we are often tempted into the mistake of reducing the phenomenon to some other, less perplexing, phenomenon that resembles it, such as, in the case of self-deception, pretence, vacillation, failure to weigh evidence correctly, etc. and in the case of weakness of will, psychic compulsion, lack of moral conviction or external coercion.

Both phenomena also produce a Psycho-Ethical Paradox of innocence together with guilt. And just as self-deception is more excusable than hypocrisy but less so than simple ignorance, weakness of will is more excusable than immoral intention but less so than genuine inner compulsion or external coercion.

The explanation I propose of both phenomena is basically the same: they are attempts to preserve the purity of the ideal self. The difference between them is this: the self-deceiver divides his *cognitive* authority between his actual and his ideal self by attempting to produce or maintain the latter's ignorance of a painful truth without forfeiting its claim to prudential and moral rationality, while the weak-willed agent divides his *volitional* authority between his actual and his ideal self, in attributing his action to the dominance of the former over the latter. Both procedures involve the pathological process of dissociation. The self-deceiver regards his projected, ideal self as an alien person whom he must deceive. The weak-willed agent, in contrast, regards his actual self as an alien force that overcomes the prudential and moral ideal with which he identifies himself (his 'real self'). This difference may explain why the self-deceiver must keep his project out of the focus of his attention (second-order self-deception), while the weak-willed person is all too eager to avow his pathological state: 'I had every intention to refuse the bribe, but I was too weak to resist it.' Frequently, they are joint aspects of the same enterprise (Sartre's examples of *mauvaise foi* are all cases where both phenomena occur). Having resolved to stop smoking, I may know very well that when presented with cigarettes I will not resist the temptation to smoke, and yet I may deceive myself into believing that I *will* resist in order to avail myself of the opportunity to succumb. Here the self-deception is about one's real intentions, as in Sartre's example of the puritanical flirt. The belated excuse of irresistible temptation is undermined by the self-deceptive strategy whereby the agent exposes himself to the tempting object.

Do the cases of weakness of will that are due to such misjudgments of one's own intentions undermine the authority of self-knowledge? On the contrary. If the phenomenon were explainable as a simple failure to understand one's own intentions or predict one's future actions, it would be completely exculpating. Yet weakness of will is a moral fault for which one is rightly condemned rather than excused. The ignorance of one's own lack of firmness of intention that leads one into temptation is not an innocent ignorance, but the product of self-deception which, as we have already noted, protects the authority of self-knowledge by dividing the actual self that knows the truth from the ideal self that is deceived. Thus both self-deception and weakness of will are exceptions to the authority of self-knowledge of that welcome kind that prove the rule.

Donald Davidson has offered an interesting new 'solution' to the Socratic paradox of *akrasia*. His 'solution' pivots on a distinction between two kinds of judgments of what is the best course of action: a *prima facie* or conditional judgment that A is the best course of action relative to all one's available reasons or evidence, and a categorical judgment that it would be best to do A *sans phrase*.[11]

While technically ingenious, Davidson's analysis seems irrelevant to the real problem of weakness of will which we have been considering, although it is helpful in revealing what is wrong with the Platonic–Aristotelian–Davidsonian *definition* of 'the problem'.

Plato characterises *akrasia* in the *Protagoras* as whether one can do evil while knowing it to be evil (where 'evil', for Plato, means what is contrary to one's long-range interest). Aristotle, in the *Nichomachean Ethics*, defines the problem similarly as whether, and, if so, how, one can act voluntarily, yet contrary to one's best judgment. Davidson defines the problem with exemplary precision, as that of whether the following three propositions are consistent:

1. If an agent wants to do $x$ more than he wants to do $y$ . . . then he will intentionally do $x$ . . .
2. If an agent judges that it would be better to do $x$ than to do $y$, then he wants to do $x$ more than he wants to do $y$.
3. There are incontinent (weak-willed) actions.

If the paradox of weakness of will were due merely to linguistic ambiguity between two sense of 'judges', as Davidson seems to maintain, then Davidson's distinction between judging best relative to all the evidence and judging best *sans phrase* would clear matters up very nicely, and no one need ever again suffer from psychic conflict. But psychic integrity, unfortunately, is not a simple function of linguistic precision. If anything, linguistic confusion is an effect, rather than a cause, of psychic conflict. The reason why descriptions of abnormal states, such as 'self-deception', 'weakness of will' and 'divided self', are paradoxical in form is that the states they describe are states of *conflict* that almost necessitate paradoxical description. Surely the reason cannot be that we are so careless in our use of language as to employ needlessly ambiguous phraseology.

The trouble with Davidson's intellectualist approach is that, like Plato and Aristotle, he attends not to the nature of the psychic conflict, but to the phraseology with which the conflict tends to be described and so proposes an escape from the verbal paradox *via* the emergency exit of disambiguation. But the fire raging in the soul of the *akrates* stays within him. Freud and Sartre realised that it is the agent himself who ignites and feeds the fire and that it is up to him to quench it by means of resolute action. There is no linguistic fire escape from internal conflicts. To resolve them, one must *act*, 'and by opposing, end them'. To believe otherwise, as Sartre noted, is self-deception.

The reader who has been patient enough to get this far may suspect that I am trying to eat my cake and have it too. I concluded the earlier discussion of self-deception by proposing that only the agent himself can resolve the paradox of belief by specifying a respect in which he believes and a different respect in which he disbelieves. Is this not a verbal resolution of a verbal paradox by means of disambiguation? To this potential accusation I must plead guilty, but with, I hope, an exonerating explanation. I do not mean to contend that paradoxes are not verbal (of course they are) but that our paradoxical descriptions of abnormal psychic life are not *merely* verbal but are reflective of genuine conflicts. Perhaps I can now make more clear the relation between resolving the psychic conflict and resolving the verbal paradox that reflects it. When the self-deceiver becomes capable of describing himself without paradox it is because he has overcome his 'cognitive dissonance', an achievement that will not be reached by language alone; he must *do* something; he must make and carry out some painful decisions. And so must the *akrates*.

It will be recalled that the metaphor of a divided self seems inescapable if we are to preserve the authority of avowals, without which there can be no language of psychology. Yet, as Sartre argued against Freud, the self cannot literally be split; to believe that it can is that very founding act of (third-order) self-deception that devotees of psychotherapy revel in. The self-deceiver splits his immediate self from his future, ideal self so that he can deceive the latter, and thereby deprives it of its *cognitive* authority. The *akrates* splits his immediate self, which he denies to be his 'real me', from his projected self in order to transfer *volitional* authority from one to the other. Both these poor wretches, if they are to be able to say non-paradoxically what they are about, must already be cured of their tendencies to do what they are doing. The 'cure' consists in (to put it tautologically but, I hope, not pointlessly) *ceasing to do* what they are doing. We might say, somewhat more pretentiously, that it consists in 'integration' of their present and future selves or egos, but to talk this way misleadingly suggests that there really are two selves. So I prefer the tautology. In brief, self-knowledge is not merely accurate and non-paradoxical self-description. It is that accurate and *honest* non-paradoxical self-description that is made possible by self-improvement.

# 8 Self and Community

'In lectures Wittgenstein imagined a tribe of people who had the idea that their slaves had no feelings, no souls – that they were automatons ... what could it mean to say that they had the idea that the slaves were automatons? Well, they would look at the slaves in a peculiar way. They would observe and comment on their movements *as if* they were machines ... They would discard them when they were worn out and useless, like machines ... Here is a difference in "attitude" that is not a matter of believing or expecting different facts' – Norman Malcolm, *Knowledge and Certainty*

If self-knowledge is authoritative in that it is not corrigible by others, how can it be a goal of psychotherapy and Socratic self-examination? The answer depends on what is meant by 'self-knowledge', which has at least three different meanings:

1. The special kind of knowledge conveyed by first-person avowals. This kind, as we have seen, is indeed authoritative, although one may forfeit his authority through insincerity, or divide it through self-deception and weakness of will.

2. Knowledge *about* oneself, that is, knowledge of one's own habits, character traits, skills and potentialities, is self-knowledge of the kind that Gilbert Ryle must have had in mind when, in *The Concept of Mind*, he insisted that others know us better than we know ourselves, and this would seem to be the kind that is sought in psychotherapy. The concept of self involved in this sense of 'self-knowledge' is the grammatical reflexive use of 'self' that we earlier discounted as trivial on the ground that it can be replaced by the name of the person. My knowledge about myself is simply my knowledge about the person I happen to be, namely, R.A., and it is acquired in the same way that my knowledge of any person is acquired – by acquaintance with that person. Needless to say, Ryle was right in denying that we have any special authority for claims to self-knowledge of this kind, other than the fact that we are, so to speak, better acquainted with ourselves, a doubtful advantage more than offset by our natural bias against recognising our own faults.

3. While the Socratic maxim 'know thyself' is often interpreted in the preceding way, as a call to self-analysis, it seems likely that Socrates was more interested in philosophical analysis than in psychoanalysis, so

that the goal he had in mind was a clearer understanding of the *idea* of self, that is, what sort of entity the self is. The value of this distinctive kind of self-knowledge is that it reveals to us wherein our true self-interest lies, and the relation between self-interest and our moral ideals. Here is where the philosophically interesting concept of self as a prudential and moral ideal becomes relevant.

The aim of this concluding chapter is to show how self-knowledge in this Socratic sense is indispensable to an adequate understanding of psychological discourse.

SELF-INTEREST AND MORALITY

In Book Two of Plato's *Republic*, Socrates is challenged by Glaucon and Adeimantus to prove that moral virtue is desirable even for one who has the 'Ring of Gyges' that renders him immune to blame and punishment. It is not quite clear whether Socrates is being asked for a proof of the coincidence of self-interest with morality, or whether he is being asked to prove that 'virtue is its own reward'. The question, 'Why should Gyges be virtuous?' can mean either 'What good will it do him?' (i.e. is it in his self-interest according to a proper understanding of the notion of self-interest?) or 'Why should Gyges place virtue above self-interest?' In a well-known essay, 'Does Moral Philosophy Rest on a Mistake?', Henry Prichard interpreted the history of ethical philosophy as an attempt to answer the second kind of question and argued that all such attempts are doomed to failure because the question is as pointless as asking why any tautology is true.[1] Kurt Baier, in *The Moral Point of View*, interpreted the question in the first sense and offered a Hobbesian account of the value to each individual of general adherence to a moral code.[2] Neither writer succeeded in putting the question to rest. Baier, like Hobbes, could explain only why it is to one's self-interest to live in a moral community, but not why one ought to follow its rules at one's own expense. Prichard rested morality on intuitive self-evidence, yet his denial of the meaningfulness of the question was contrary to our intuition that the question is meaningful. Perhaps their common mistake was to accept the popular notion of self-interest as contrary to morality. More recently, Alan Gewirth and Thomas Nagel have suggested that an adequate analysis of self-interest shows it to be consistent with the demands of moral obligation. John Rawls, proceeding from a different direction, has arrived at the same conclusion. While there are lacunae in the reasoning of all three writers, due to an insufficient account of the concepts of person and self, I think that their conclusion is sound and that the results arrived at in our present study provide the needed grounds for that conclusion.

In an essay entitled, 'Must We Play the Moral Language Game?', Alan Gewirth has argued that rational judgments of prudential self-interest entail moral obligations:

... Anyone who accepts ... universal statements as personal-prescriptive ones endorsing the end as well as the means ... must also accept the singular statement, 'I ought to refrain from interfering with other persons doing z if they want to have y.' Hence, on the basis of his own self-interested acts and judgments, X must uphold a system of mutual rights and duties in which his 'ought'-judgments in support of his own freedom of action entail further 'ought'-judgments in which he accords similar freedom to others.[3]

Gewirth's argument is that any self-interested singular 'ought'-judgment entails a universal 'ought'-judgment about what anyone in the same circumstances as oneself ought to do, and that this latter judgment entails the obligation not to interfere with the action thus prescribed. These entailments, he claims, follow from the concept of a reason for action:

It is a logical feature of all reasons that they are implicitly general, referring to a general rule or principle that serves to ground the connection asserted in the particular case.[4]

Gewirth assumes without proof that a prudential or self-interested reason for an action must take the form of a singular 'ought'-judgment: I ought to do A to get B. He then argues that this entails a universal 'ought'-judgment to the effect that everyone ought to do A to get B. But he does not explain why a prudential reason must take the form of a singular 'ought'-judgment. What have reasons for action to do with obligations? For the answer to this question, we must turn from Gewirth to Nagel.

In *The Possibility of Altruism*, Thomas Nagel has explained the connection between prudential reasons and judgments of moral obligation in terms of the relation between what he calls the 'personal' and 'impersonal standpoints'. Nagel distinguishes 'subjective reasons' for action that make essential reference to a particular agent (usually, although not necessarily oneself) as beneficiary of the action, from 'objective reasons' that specify value or benefit for any agent in virtue of which he ought to perform the action that produces the benefit. Nagel then argues that to be motivated by subjective reasons alone involves a dissociation between the personal and impersonal standpoints, a dissociation that he aptly characterises as 'practical solipsism'. If one is indifferent to objective reasons, then, when he considers his own interests and alternative courses of action impersonally, he will be indifferent toward them; they will not have the motivating force of reasons. Only when he sees interests as *his* interests will they have such force. Nagel concludes that a-moral egoism of this sort is an expression of a split personality, a kind of ethical schizophrenia:

The fact is that neither of the two standpoints can be eliminated from our view of the world, and when one of them cannot accept the judgments of the other, we are faced with a situation in which the individual is not operating as a unit. Two sides of the idea of himself, and hence two sides of himself, are coming apart. The only principles which avoid this result in the practical sphere are objective ones.[5]

Nagel's argument sounds more psychological and thus more contingent than I think it is intended to be. It sounds as if we are merely being warned that it is imprudent to reject the claims of morality because doing so will make us lonely and unhappy solipsists. But I do not think that this psychological truism is what Nagel is really driving at. I think he means to claim that the dissociation of standpoints involved in 'practical solipsism' is not merely undesirable, but conceptually absurd, and that it is impossible to hold such a position consistently, because the *self* in the self-interest of the a-moral egoist has vanished, and with it, his self-interest as well. Why and how this occurs will be considered below.

In Part Three of his influential work, *A Theory of Justice*, John Rawls reasons in the reverse direction from Gewirth and Nagel, attempting to derive prudence from morality along Kantian lines, rather than deriving morality from prudence. Prudence is explained as a duty to oneself, following from our natural duties to all persons:

...We have the guiding principle that a rational individual is always to act so that he need never blame himself no matter how his plans finally work out. Viewing himself as one continuing being over time, he can say that at each moment of his life he has done what the balance of reasons required, or at least permitted.[6]

...Now looked at in this way, the principle of responsibility to self resembles a principle of right; the claims of the self at different times are to be so adjusted that the self at each time can affirm the plan that has been and is being followed. The person at one time, so to speak, must not be able to complain about actions of the person at another time.[7]

Rawls thus assimilates the motivational force of prudential rationality to that of moral rationality. We owe it to ourselves to act on the best reasons because we owe this to everyone. But in taking this view, Rawls would seem to have inherited the moral austerity of Kant with its attendant faults. The idea that one has duties and obligations to oneself as well as to others asserts too strong a bond between prudence and morality, one that is plainly counter-intuitive. We do not really regard

ourselves as committing moral offences when we neglect or mistreat
ourselves; we speak this way at times, but in a metaphorical tone of
voice, to make a point by deliberate exaggeration. Clearly one has a
right to inject himself with a dangerous virus in order to find an
immunising vaccine, or to sacrifice himself for a higher cause; such
people are considered heroic, not criminal. Yet one does not have the
same right to sacrifice others, no matter how noble the purpose. The
idea of moral duties toward oneself overstates the degree of symmetry
between the demands of prudence and those of morality, just as
a-moral egoism overstates the a-symmetry.

Nevertheless it is an interesting fact that we so often speak of duties
toward ourselves and that we think of self-indulgence and self-neglect
as moral vices. But this fact can be explained without going as far as
Kant and Rawls in eradicating the difference between prudence and
morality. Our earlier discussion of the origin and role of the ideal self
provides an alternative explanation. One's ideal self, which one is often
tempted to reify into an actual person with whom one must come to
terms and satisfy, plays the role of another person toward whom one
then appears to have duties and obligations. In the passage cited,
Rawls speaks of 'the claims of self' in just this manner, as if a person
and his 'self' were two entities having toward each other the moral
relations of rights and duties. As we have seen, our temptation to take
this figure of speech literally is one of the sources of self-deception; the
main reason why we feel it necessary to deceive ourselves is that we feel
it necessary to answer to something in us that plays the role of judge of
our actions. The notion of duties to ourselves when taken literally,
however, is as paradoxical as that of self-deception and for the same
reason: the relation of being obligated toward, like that of deception,
is irreflexive, requiring non-identical relata.

The fact is, however, that we do not have to give ourselves justifying
reasons for action by engaging in inward debates and sophistical
strategies. Contrary to Gewirth's assumption, the a-moralist need not
ever formulate singular ought-judgments to guide his actions, providing he is willing to pay the price indicated by Nagel of dissociating his
personal from his impersonal standpoint. And many are obviously
willing to pay that price. But that we so often do engage in inward
interrogation and in self-deception shows that we sense some connection
between prudence and morality, while the fact that we need not play
this game shows that the connection is not, as Rawls seems to claim, as
simple as that of instantiation between particular duties and general
duties.

I have said that while we often give ourselves reasons for action, we
need not do so. What I mean is this: it was pointed out earlier in this
study (Chapter 4) that certain locutions that look like reason-giving
locutions are, in fact, reason-terminating, because they give us to

understand that the action in question is not in need of rational justification. For example, when I am asked why I am going to the movies
and I reply 'Because I want to', I am not trying to justify myself;
rather, I am informing my questioner that his question is out of order.
The general point that this use of reason-terminating locutions brings
to light is that the enterprise of offering reasons for and against actions
is a social, not a personal activity, the need for it arising only when, as
R. S. Peters put it, the agent violates or at least appears to violate some
rule or customary expectation and is therefore called to account. Now
this sort of procedure is not normally appropriate to prudential
deliberation on what to do to achieve one's personal goals. When I
deliberate on what to do in my own self-interest, I need not add the
motivational force of 'ought' to my judgment as to what is best for me,
since I am already sufficiently motivated in favour of my long-range
interests. Deliberation on what I *ought* to do is more than prudential;
it is a rehearsal for self-justification before the court of persons-in-
general, that is, the moral community, and thus it makes sense only if I
have already adopted the 'moral point of view' and am already concerned about the propriety of my actions. Thus even the prudential
'ought' need not concern the avowed a-moralist. He is not interested in
self-justification. The trick is to prove to him that he *should* be interested.

We can now see more clearly the merit in Gewirth's assumption
that there is a logical connection between prudential reasons and
obligations. If the a-moralist is not interested in justification, what
would be the point of his giving *reasons* for his actions, either to others
or to himself? Does even the concept of self-interest play any real role
in his deliberations on what to do? We found earlier that the non-
trivial concept of self is a moral ideal, and that giving reasons is a move
in the game of justification and excuse. Both notions, therefore, to
apply at all, presuppose a moral community of persons, of which the
agent is one member among others. His self-interest, as Gewirth and
Nagel point out, is a *reason* for action only as an instance of interests
in general, for the very function of the idea of having an interest is to
provide a *prima facie* reason for an action. Thus the concept of self-
interest has a use only in a moral community in which the interests of
persons are weighed against each other as competing reasons for action.
Self-interest therefore cannot be conceived in total independence of
moral constraints without rendering vacuous the concepts of self,
interest and reasons.

The degree of tightness of the bond between self-interest and morality
can be located in the notion of the ideal self. Each person's ideal self is
unique (for one reason, because it essentially involves his body, which
is unique, and for another, because no two value systems are identical),
yet all such ideals of self share a common denominator in the mutual

recognition of interests as reasons for action. Without that mutual recognition, the concepts of person, self and reason would have no application, nor would the concept of moral obligation. Nevertheless, it is not to be expected that a person will assign exactly the same weight to the interests of another that he assigns to his own. Since interests are reasons for action, and a person is primarily responsible only for his own actions, his own interests may legitimately have preferential weight *for his own actions*, and his understanding of what it is to be a person should make it clear to him that the same is true, *mutatis mutandis*, for other persons. The reason why a person does not literally have duties toward himself is that, as the authority on his own interests, he has the right to give more weight to one interest, say the advancement of science, than to another such as his own health or his own life. But he has no such authority over the relative weights of the interests of others.

Every person has an interest in maintaining his rights against encroachment, and thus in maintaining a moral community that recognises and protects such rights. Thus as Baier, following Hobbes, has emphasised, conformity to moral rules enhances the self-interest of the members of a community. However, this still does not explain how it is to the self-interest of an individual to refrain from immoral action that, because of successful concealment, as in the case of Gyges, will not endanger the sense of mutual trust essential to preservation of a moral community.

The more intimate bond we are seeking between self-interest and moral duty is to be found in the concept of self. The ideal self, whose interests one aims at fulfilling, incorporates his moral principles, one of which is the principle of mutual respect for interests. So that if self-interest is understood as the interest of the *ideal* self, it follows that the fulfilment of one's moral values is to his self-interest. But do we not ordinarily mean, by 'self-interest', that which promotes the goals of the *actual* self? No doubt we do, which is why writers like Prichard assume that self-interest and moral duty are generally incompatible. But once we distinguish the actual from the ideal self, it becomes clear that our ordinary use of 'self-interest', which presupposes an identity of the two senses of 'self', does not apply to this predicament of a divided self. For given this division, where one's prudential and moral values belong to one's ideal self as set apart from one's actual self, what remains of the actual self is – nothing at all, other than the mere grammatically reflexive role of referring to the subject of a sentence, the use that a computer can make of 'self' as well as a person. As Nagel points out, this trivial use of 'self' does not even involve continuity through time, so that considerations of prudence as well as those of morality transcend this trivial sense of 'self', which has no rational interests at all. Thus while the a-moral egoist cannot be refuted, neither can he claim to have a non-trivial concept of self in terms of which he can speak intelligibly of his self-interest, and thus of his reasons for action. The price of consistency for him is therefore the same as the price of consistency for the scientific determinist. Both must eschew the language-game of reasons for action, and thus dispense not only with ethics, but with psychology as well. Both have reduced themselves and others to programmed automata, non-persons, with no self other than that of grammatical reflexivity. As Wittgenstein says of the solipsist, the self has shrunk to a dimensionless point, i.e. to nothing.

The concepts of person, self and reason for action are thus bound together by a commitment to mutual recognition of interests that defines a moral community. Persons can and do have substantive moral codes that differ in the specific types of interests they pursue and in their order of priorities, and thus have different ideal selves. The Christian makes salvation his paramount goal, the hedonist stresses pleasure, the Buddhist amelioration of suffering, the patriot national power. Nonetheless, if they are to be able to understand each other psychologically, and live together in one community, they must engage in the enterprise of justification in terms of commonly accepted reasons, and thus agree on the moral principle that each person's interest counts as a reason for action, and that in the absence of hypocrisy or self-deception, a person's avowals of his interests are authoritative. Social justice and political democracy, as John Rawls has argued in *A Theory of Justice*, are the application of this principle to the institutional structure of society.

The fact that individuals have different systems of relative values explains why, even from the standpoint of an ideal self, self-interest is not identical with morality. But the fact that the concept of a person entails a community of persons who acknowledge each other's interests as reasons for actions explains why self-interest must be defined as consistent with the interests of others and thus with morality.

Philosophers who have commented on the meaning of life or the nature of self-fulfilment have tended to overemphasise either the autonomous or the heteronomous aspect of person-status to the detriment of the other. Nietzscheans and existentialists have emphasised autonomy – the freedom of the individual to define his own values and, in so doing, to give his life whatever meaning it has. Religious writers, Hegelians and Marxists have emphasised the heteronomous conditions they regard as essential to being a person, consisting in the cosmic or historical pattern within which the life of the individual acquires significance. We have seen that the concept of a person necessarily involves both aspects. One cannot be a subject of psychological predication without the freedom to act on reasons independently of causes, and without the authority to avow one's feelings, emotions, intentions and goals. But equally, one cannot have the status of a person without other persons who acknowledge that status and understand one's avowed reasons because, to some extent, they share them.

CONCLUSIONS

Our investigations of the logic of psychological discourse have uncovered entities and properties that seem a far cry from what scientific psychologists believe to lie within their purview. We found in Chapter 2 that the public incorrigibility of avowals, which explains the distinctive psychological features of intentionality, normative judgment and non-observational self-knowledge, is an authority bestowed on us by society in acknowledging our status as persons. Considerations of the logic of motivational concepts, in Chapters 3 and 4, disclosed that the explanation of actions in terms of reasons provides the grounds for evaluating the actions rather than deducing them from causes. Ascriptions of emotions and desires were found to involve normative judgments of eliciting circumstances and appropriate responses. In Chapter 5 we examined the claims of mind–body theories that attempt to dispense with reasons in favour of causes and we found them to be incoherent. In Chapter 6 psychological predicates were seen to apply only to persons as subjects. Person status was found not to be reducible to any set of necessary and sufficient psychological predicates because the latter presuppose person-status which, as a subject of rights and responsibilities, is supervenient to its descriptive criteria. We distinguished the social status of being a person from the concept of an ideal self with which a person identifies the fulfilment of his paramount goals and interests. This concept of an ideal self enabled us in Chapter 7 to untangle the paradoxes of self-deception while preserving the authority of self-knowledge and, in this concluding chapter, to vindicate the Socratic insistence on the compatibility of self-interest with moral obligation.

The aim of this study has been to show that man has a psycho-ethical dimension not reducible to biological and physical processes, that to live as a human being is to be a member of a moral community of autonomous persons, a free and rational author of actions and avowals, who assumes responsibilities toward other persons in respecting their equal authority. In ascribing feelings, emotions and reasons to himself and to others, he forms an ideal of himself which it is the purpose of his life to fulfil, and only insofar as his ideal self shares a common moral ground with the ideals of other persons, can he hope to understand them and to be understood.

# Notes

## Chapter 1

1 'Psychology is fundamentally a biological science, not a social science ...', D. O. Hebb, *A Textbook of Psychology* (Philadelphia: W. B. Saunders, 1958) preface.
2 G. E. M. Anscombe, *Intention* (Oxford: Blackwell, 1957) sect. 8; P. F. Strawson, *Individuals* (London: Methuen, 1959) ch. iii; Sidney Shoemaker, *Self Knowledge and Self Identity* (Ithaca: Cornell University Press, 1963) pp. 214 f.; N. Malcolm, 'Behaviorism as a Philosophy of Psychology', in *Behaviorism and Phenomenology*, ed. T. W. Wann (University of Chicago Press, 1964).
3 R. S. Peters, *The Concept of Motivation* (New York: Humanities Press, 1958) ch. ii; P. Winch, *The Idea of a Social Science* (New York: Humanities Press, 1958).
4 Gilbert Ryle, *The Concept of Mind* (New York: Barnes & Noble, 1949) pp. 130 f., on 'achievement verbs'.
5 R. Chisholm, 'Sentences about Believing', *Proceedings of the Aristotelian Society*, 56 (1955–6); reprinted in Feigl, Scriven and Maxwell (eds), *Minnesota Studies in the Philosophy of Science* (Minneapolis: University of Minnesota Press, 1958) vol. ii, appendix.
6 E. Nagel, *The Structure of Science* (New York: Harcourt, Brace & World, 1961) chs 2–3. Nagel recognises teleological and genetic types of explanation, but maintains that they are reducible to deductive and probabilistic types. See also C. G. Hempel and P. Oppenheim, 'The Logic of Explanation', *Philosophy of Science* (1948) for an equally influential statement of this view.
7 S. Shoemaker, op. cit. pp. 230 f.
8 A. C. MacIntyre, *The Unconscious* (New York: Humanities Press, 1957) pp. 48 f.

## Chapter 2

1 In J. L. Austin's sense of 'performative', in *How to do Things With Words* (Oxford: Oxford University Press, 1965) p. 6.
2 Anscombe, op. cit. and P. F. Strawson, *Individuals* (London: Methuen, 1959; New York: Doubleday Anchor, 1963) ch. iii.
3 Chisholm, op. cit.
4 A. I. Melden, *Free Action* (London: Routledge & Kegan Paul; New York: Humanities Press, 1961); R. Taylor, *Action and Purpose* (Englewood Cliffs: Prentice-Hall, 1966); C. Taylor, *The Explanation of Behavior* (London: Routledge & Kegan Paul, 1964); Peters, op. cit.

5 Cf. B. Aune, to whom I owe this argument, in *Knowledge, Mind, and Nature* (New York: Random House, 1967) pp. 88 f.

6 It might be objected that I can misidentify myself as R.A. when I say that R.A. weighs 150 pounds, just as well as when I say that R.A. loves you. But by 'replaceable by the speaker's name or any definite description of him', I mean any way that enables the listener to identify the subject, whether that name or description belongs to him or not. In such case, the truth conditions do not change (even where I am wrong about my name) as they would, say, if, while thinking I was depressing the scale at 150, someone else really was. (I owe this correction to Meredith Swenson.)

7 This account is, I think, subtly hinted at, although not explicitly developed, by Stuart Hampshire, in *Freedom of the Individual* (New York: Harper & Row, 1965), esp. ch. 4.

8 J. Fodor, *Psychological Explanation* (New York: Random House, 1968).

9 By 'ability' I do not mean the mere absence of disability of the kind exemplified by the deaf-mute in my example, but the more complex and positive concept of capacity or skill.

10 R. Rorty, 'Mind-Body Identity, Privacy and Categories', *The Review of Metaphysics*, 19 (1965) 24–54.

11 L. Wittgenstein, *Philosophical Investigations*, trans. G. Anscombe (New York: Macmillan, 1953) p. 244.

## Chapter 3

1 To forestall misunderstanding, may I remind the reader that in this context I mean by 'indeterminism' not the absence of a possible cause, but the senselessness of *either* causal attribution or causal denial; in brief, the inapplicability of causal language.

2 Ryle, op. cit. p. 113.

3 Ibid. pp. 113–14.

4 W. Dray, *Laws and Explanation in History* (Oxford: Oxford University Press, 1957) pp. 150–5.

5 Melden, op. cit. p. 77.

6 Ibid. p. 88.

7 Dray, op. cit. p. 126.

8 Melden, op. cit. p. 102.

9 Ibid. p. 104.

10 Peters, op. cit. pp. 35–6.

11 G. E. M. Anscombe and Philippa Foot have argued that a motive need not be a character trait in Ryle's sense of a *permanent* disposition. But a motive must relate action to character in *some* way. How do we know that Smith's motive was revenge? He need not be generally vindictive, but he must at least have some general trait (jealousy, vanity, or such) which makes it plausible to ascribe to him the motive of revenge in a particular situation. Anscombe, op. cit. p. 21; P. Foot, 'Free Will as Involving Determinism', in *The Philosophical Review*, 64 (1957).

12 Cf. Peters, op. cit. p. 7.

13 R. Taylor, op. cit. pp. xiv, 269.

14 It is difficult to specify this sense of 'cause' to everyone's satisfaction but

it can at least be said that, for determinism to be non-trivial, a cause must be a *sufficient* condition, not just a necessary one (e.g. breathing is hardly the deterministic cause of painting a masterpiece) and not just any old answer to the question 'Why?'

15 'This by itself shows that the relation expressed in the hypothetical, "I will move my finger if I want to", is...a logical relationship between concepts...and, as such, cannot be a causal relationship between states or events' (p. 52). Also p. 72, '...decisions, choices, desires...and the like serve no better than volitions as the causes of actions and for precisely the same reason – namely, that it is impossible...even to begin to say what these events are without describing them in terms of their alleged effects'.

16 Cf. D. Davidson, 'Actions, Reasons and Causes', in *Journal of Philosophy*, 60, no. 23 (1963) pp. 685–700; R. Brandt and J. Kim, 'Wants as Explanation of Actions', *Journal of Philosophy*, 60, no. 15 (1963) pp. 425–35; C. G. Hempel, 'Reasons and Covering Laws in Historical Explanation', in *Philosophy and History*, ed. S. Hook (New York: New York University Press, 1963) pp. 143–63; B. Goldberg, 'Can a Desire be a Cause?', in *Analysis*, 25, no. 3 (1965) pp. 70–2; B. Berofsky, 'Determinism and the Concept of a Person', in *Journal of Philosophy*, 61 (1964) pp. 461–75 (esp. p. 474); W. D. Gean, 'Reasons and Causes', in *Review of Metaphysics*, 19, no. 4 (1966) pp. 667–88; J. Margolis, *Psychotherapy and Morality* (New York: Random House, 1966) ch. 4; A. Kaplan, *The Conduct of Inquiry* (San Francisco: Chandler, 1964) pp. 115–25; A. C. MacIntyre, 'The Antecedents of Action', in *British Analytical Philosophy*, ed. B. Williams and A. Montefiore (New York: Humanities Press; London: Routledge & Kegan Paul, 1966) pp. 205–25.

17 Davidson, op. cit. p. 696.

18 Goldberg, op. cit.

19 Davidson, op. cit. p. 696.

20 *Vide* ch. 6.

21 Gean, op. cit. *passim*.

22 Ibid. pp. 669–75.

23 Ibid. p. 674.

24 Contention (3) is, properly interpreted, perfectly correct, but the trouble is, as we shall see, that Taylor misinterprets it as compatible with determinism.

25 Cf. Melden, op. cit. ch. 9; R. Taylor, op. cit. pp. 73 f., C. Taylor, op. cit.

26 'If we compare this [a mere bodily event] with some act, such as the act of moving my hand, then however detailed the description, we shall not describe it as an act until we state that some agent has caused it' (p. 109). This seems clearly to assert that an agent is the cause of his *act*, not simply of an event brought about by his act. But later he says: 'Unlike the match, the man can bring about such a change as a motion of his arm quite by himself,' (p. 122) and he then claims that 'I move my finger' entails 'Something makes my finger move' (p. 123). Finally, 'There is an essential reference to the agent as the cause of the *motion*' (p. 125, my italics).

27 Cf. A. C. Danto's illuminating analyses of the difference between 'basic' and 'non-basic' actions in 'What We Can Do', *Journal of Philosophy*, 60, (1963) pp. 435–45, and 'Freedom and Forebearance', in *Freedom*

*and Determinism,* ed. K. Lehrer (New York: Random House, 1966) pp. 45–63.

28 Ibid. pp. 143–4.
29 Ibid. p. 146.
30 Ibid. p. 114.
31 Ibid. p. 151.
32 E.g., André Schwartzbart's moving historical novel, *The Last of the Just,* Gibbon's *Decline and Fall of the Roman Empire,* describing the enthusiastic martyrdom of the early Christians, B. Souverine's description, in his biography of Stalin, of the Bolshevik terrorist, Kamo, and Henri Alleg's account of the torture of pro-Algerians in *La Question.*

*Chapter 4*

1 K. Baier, *The Moral Point of View* (Ithaca: Cornell University Press, 1958) pp. 108 ff.
2 Nevertheless, as I shall later try to show, there is a good deal of truth in Ryle's account.
3 Melden, op. cit. pp. 161–2; P. H. Nowell-Smith, *Ethics* (Oxford: Blackwell, 1957) pp. 130 ff.
4 Peters, op. cit. p. 29.
5 I owe this point to Professor P. Bennett's doctoral dissertation in defence of compatibilism (New York University, 1971).
6 Cf. A. Kenny, *Action, Emotion and Will* (London: Routledge & Kegan Paul; New York: Humanities Press, 1963) p. 115.
7 Cf. my 'A Spade is a Spade', in *Dimensions of Mind,* ed. Hook.
8 Cf. Peters, op. cit. p. 17.
9 T. Nagel, *The Possibility of Altruism* (New York: Oxford University Press, 1970) ch. VI.
10 Cf. E. Duffy, 'An Explanation of "Emotional" Phenomena Without the Use of the Concept "Emotion"': 'Change in energy levels appears to be the most characteristic feature of the condition called "emotion"' (p. 25); P. T. Young, 'Methods for the Study of Feeling and Emotion': 'An emotion is a natural event. It is something that happens, as does a thunderstorm or sunrise.' (p. 271) and 'An emotion is an acute disturbance of the individual' (p. 72); K. M. B. Bridges, 'Emotional Development in Early Infancy',: 'The emotional reactions of the tiny infant are certainly not highly differentiated. The most common response to highly stimulating situations seems to be one of general agitation or excitement.' (p. 104) in *Emotion: Bodily Change,* ed. D. K. Candland (Princeton, N.J.: Van Nostrand, 1962). Also Hebb, op. cit. p. 156: 'We may think of "emotion" therefore as more a common sense than a psychological term; what it appears to mean is, crudely, that something exceptional is going on in the individual.' Hebb identifies 'these goings on' with 'irritability' and 'overflow response'. Also Galanter, Mandler, Brown and Hess (eds), *New Directions in Psychology* (New York: Holt, Rinehart & Winston, 1962) p. 46: 'Miller, Galanter and Pribram (1960) have suggested that this sort of homeostatic mechanism is the general model for goal directed behavior ...'

11 Cf. Peters, op. cit. ch. III.

12 E. Bedford, 'Emotions', reprinted from *Proceedings of the Aristotelian Society* in *Essays in Philosophical Psychology*, ed. D. Gustafson (Garden City: Anchor Books, 1964).

13 J.-P. Sartre, *The Emotions, Outline of a Theory*, trans. B. Frechtman (New York: Philosophical Library, 1948).

14 Recall that a person's reasons are dependent on his beliefs and values. They are *allegations* of facts or rules as premises for a judgment, and need not be true. That is why not all reasons need be good reasons, and why actions are subject to public criticism.

15 This is not to agree with Pascal's romantic paradox: '*Le coeur a ses raisons que le raison ne connait pas*', but rather that 'reasons of the heart', i.e. reasons that evoke emotions such as anger, love, fear and joy, may be very good reasons from the standpoint of both self-interest and the common good.

16 Cf. T. S. Szasz, *The Myth of Mental Illness* (New York: Hoeber-Harper, 1961); R. D. Laing, *The Divided Self* (Baltimore: Pelican Books, 1965); J. H. Van den Berg, *The Phenomenological Approach to Psychiatry* (Springfield: Thomas, 1955).

17 Harvey Mullane, 'Psychoanalytic Explanation and Rationality', *Journal of Philosophy*, 68, no. 14 (1971).

18 Op. cit. p. 423.

19 Ibid. p. 421.

20 Ibid. p. 426.

*Chapter 5*

1 Op. cit. p. 201.

2 Cf. Melden, op. cit. p. 68.

3 Although the physical *event*, the upward motion of the hand, remains, of course, the later effect of the earlier cause consisting in the brain events $B_n$.

4 Descartes made an inconsistent exception for acts of will, which he was unable to square with the rest of his metaphysics.

5 We do sometimes (though not as often as many philosophers assume) gradually by deliberation, 'frame a decision', 'form an intention', 'make up our minds', etc. But, aside from preparatory actions (including giving ourselves instructions), these 'mental processes' are purely metaphorical, in view of the logical connection argument of Chapter 3.

6 See, for example, H. Feigl, 'Mind–Body, Not a Pseudoproblem', in *Dimensions of Mind*, ed. Sidney Hook (New York: New York University Press, 1960) and *The 'Mental' and the 'Physical'* (Minneapolis: University of Minnesota Press, 1967), reprinted from *Minnesota Studies in the Philosophy of Science*, vol. II, ed. H. Feigl, M. Scriven and G. Maxwell (University of Minnesota Press, 1958); T. Nagel, 'Physicalism', *Philosophical Review*, 74 (1965) 339–56; R. Rorty, op. cit. pp. 24–54; J. J. C. Smart, 'Materialism', *Journal of Philosophy*, 60–2 (1963) 651–2. I am grateful to Professor Feigl for his helpful comments and criticism of earlier drafts.

7 I italicise 'possible' to avoid the irrelevant objection that the number of *actual* mental states of an organism is finite, and that we need concern ourselves only with actual states. The reason this objection is irrelevant is that the identity theorist surely wants to claim, not just that all *past* mental states have been identical with bodily states, but also that all future states will also satisfy this condition. Now all possible mental states are candidates for future actual states, since there is no reason to assume that any particular mental state will never occur. Moreover, any one of the infinite number of possible mental states may be occurring right now, in some thinking organism, and if so, then according to the theory of mind–body identity, there is also some bodily state occurring which is identical with that mental state. But for this to be logically possible, the number of possible bodily states must be at least as great as the number of possible mental states.

8 I say, 'used to think', because the actual relation I have in mind between thoughts and brain states is that the latter are the *instruments* by means of which a person thinks his thoughts. I am enough of a materialist (on empirical grounds) to believe that brain events are necessary instruments of thoughts, but not that they are sufficient conditions. The relation between the thinking person and his brain states is like that between the operator of a computer and the states of the computer. The operator uses the computer states to solve a problem. The solution is not identical with the state of the computer by means of which the problem is solved. In brief, the relation between brain states and thoughts is not the relation of identity, but that of means to ends. And this relation is, of course, many-many.

9 From a letter to me by Professor Feigl. I am grateful for his kind permission to quote from this.

10 I owe this suggestion to my colleague, Chauncey Downes, and also to Professor Feigl in his correspondence with me.

11 H. Putnam, 'Minds and Machines', in *Dimensions of Mind*, ed. Hook, 'Brains and Behavior', in *Analytical Philosophy*, second series, ed. R. J. Butler (Oxford: Blackwell, 1965), and 'Psychological Predicates', in *Art, Mind, and Religion*, ed. W. H. Capitan (Pittsburgh: University of Pittsburgh Press, 1968).

12 'Comments', in *Art, Mind, and Religion*, ed. Capitan, p. 50.

13 S. Kripke, 'Naming and Necessity', *Semantics of Natural Language*, ed. D. Davidson and G. Harman (New York: Humanities Press, 1972) and 'Identity and Necessity', in *Identity and Individuation*, ed. M. K. Munitz (New York University Press, 1971).

*Chapter 6*

1 Shoemaker, op. cit. chs I and II.

2 Ibid. p. 258.

3 Strawson, op. cit. ch. 3.

4 Ibid. ch. 3.

5 A. J. Ayer, *The Concept of a Person and other Essays* (New York: St Martin's Press, 1963) p. 95: 'But what exactly is meant here by saying

that a criterion is logically adequate? Not that the evidence entails the conclusion, for in that case we should not stop short of physicalism. Not that the evidence provides sufficient empirical support for the conclusion, for then the reasoning is inductive; we are back with the argument from analogy. What is envisaged is something between the two but what can this be? What other possibility remains?'

6 Strawson, op. cit. p. 109.

7 I am suggesting that being a person, that is, being a subject to whom it makes sense to attribute any p-predicates, is a contextual presupposition for the ascription to an entity of a particular p-predicate. This, I think, is the meaning of the remark of Wittgenstein quoted at the beginning of this chapter.

8 Strawson explicitly warns: 'Of course these remarks are not intended to suggest how the problem of other minds can be solved' (op. cit. p. 109).

9 On the element of choice in deciding whether to extend person-status to non-humans, cf. H. Putnam's interesting discussion in 'Minds and Machines', *Dimensions of Mind*, ed. Hook, and in 'Robots: Machines or Artificially Created Life?', *Journal of Philosophy*, 61 (1964).

10 R. Carnap, 'Testability and Meaning', *Philosophy of Science*, 3 (1963) pt. I.

11 Cf. Ryle, op. cit. ch. v.

12 A. Kenny, *Action*, op. cit. pp. 67 f.

13 R. M. Hare, *The Language of Morals* (Oxford: Clarendon Press, 1952) ch. II; W. B. Gallie, 'Essentially Contested Concepts', *Proceedings of the Aristotelian Society*, 56 (1956).

14 Cf. A. C. Danto, 'Human Nature and Natural Law', in *Law and Philosophy*, ed. S. Hook (New York University Press, 1964).

15 Shoemaker, op. cit.; T. Penelhum, *Survival and Disembodied Existence* (New York: Humanities Press, 1970).

16 Not to be confused with assembly line production, where one sells only one's labour time so that 'work' means only activity, not the product of activity, in which case the problem is not so much 'alienation' from *oneself* as it is that of a resulting impoverishment of self.

17 R. D. Laing, 'Ontological Insecurity', in *Psychoanalysis and Existential Philosophy*, ed. H. M. Ruitenbeek (New York: Dutton, 1962).

18 In some cases, they may vary inversely, as Sartre illustrates by the waiter who has so lively a sense of his social identity as a waiter that he has lost the sense of himself as subject of action and desire.

*Chapter 7*

1 S. Freud, *The Ego and the Id*, trans. J. Riviere (New York: Norton, 1960) ch. II; *A General Introduction to Psychoanalysis*, trans. J. Riviere (New York: Washington Square Press, 1960) First Lecture.

2 J.-P. Sartre, *Being and Nothingness*, trans. H. Barnes (New York: Pocket Books, 1966) pt I, ch. II.

3 Ibid. 'Under these conditions what can be the significance of the ideal of sincerity except as a task impossible to achieve, of which the very meaning is in contradiction with the structure of my consciousness.' (p. 105)

'What then is sincerity except precisely a phenomenon of bad faith?'
(p. 107) 'Every belief is a belief that falls short; one never wholly believes
what one believes.' (p. 115)

4 H. Fingarette, *Self Deception* (New York: Humanities Press, 1968).

5 Ibid. chs 3 and 4.

6 Ryle, op. cit. ch. VI, sec. 7.

7 Freud, *Group Psychology and Analysis of the Ego* (London, 1922).

8 Sartre, op. cit. pt 4, chs I and III.

9 It is a provocative feature of orthodox psychoanalysis, as Sartre noted,
that instead of providing philosophical therapy (clarity) by helping the
patient to see the metaphysical mischief of regarding himself as an alien
person, that is, as an object of self-scrutiny deprived of the authority of
non-observational self-knowledge, orthodox psychoanalysis fosters the very
illusion that lies at the source of neurosis, the illusion that one can be at
the same time subject and object of observation.

10 H. Johnstone, *The Problem of the Self* (Pennsylvania State College Press,
1970).

11 D. Davidson, 'How is Weakness of the Will Possible?', in *Moral Problems*,
ed. J. Feinberg (Oxford: Oxford University Press, 1969).

*Chapter 8*

1 H. A. Prichard, 'Does Moral Philosophy Rest on a Mistake?', *Mind*
(1912).

2 K. Baier, op. cit.

3 A. Gewirth, 'Must We Play the Moral Language Game?', *American
Philosophical Quarterly*, 7 (1970) 116.

4 Ibid. p. 112.

5 T. Nagel, *The Possibility of Altruism*, p. 119.

6 J. Rawls, *A Theory of Justice* (Cambridge, Mass.: Harvard University
Press, 1971) p. 422.

7 Ibid. p. 423.

# Selected Bibliography

BOOKS

Anscombe, G. E. M., *Intention* (Oxford: Blackwell, 1957).
Armstrong, D. M., *A Materialist Theory of Mind* (New York: Humanities Press, 1968).
Aune, B., *Knowledge, Mind and Nature* (New York: Random House, 1967).
Austin, J. L., *How to Do Things With Words* (Oxford: Oxford University Press, 1965).
Ayer, A. J., *The Concept of a Person and other Essays* (London: Macmillan, 1963; New York: St Martin's Press, 1963).
Baier, K., *The Moral Point of View* (Ithaca: Cornell University Press, 1958).
Berofsky, B., *Determinism* (Princeton, N.J.: Princeton University Press, 1971).
Butler, R. J. (ed.), *Analytical Philosophy*, 2nd ser. (Oxford: Blackwell, 1965).
Candland, D. K. (ed.), *Emotion: Bodily Change* (Princeton, N.J.: Van Nostrand, 1962).
Capitan, W. H. (ed.), *Art, Mind and Religion* (Pittsburgh: Pittsburgh University Press, 1968).
Danto, A. C., *An Analytical Philosophy of Action* (Cambridge: Cambridge University Press, 1973).
Dray, W., *Laws and Explanation in History* (Oxford: Oxford University Press, 1957).
Feigl, H. and Scriven, M. (eds), *Minnesota Studies in the Philosophy of Science*, vol. I (Minneapolis: University of Minnesota Press, 1956).
Feigl, H., Scriven, M. and Maxwell, G. (eds), *Minnesota Studies in the Philosophy of Science*, vol. II (1958).
Feinberg, J. (ed.), *Moral Problems* (Oxford: Oxford University Press, 1969).
—— *Doing and Deserving* (Princeton, N.J.: Princeton University Press, 1970).
Fingarette, H., *Self Deception* (New York: Humanities Press, 1968).
Fodor, J., *Psychological Explanation* (New York: Random House, 1968).
Freud, S., *The Ego and the Id*, trans. J. Riviere (New York: Norton, 1960).
—— *A General Introduction to Psychoanalysis*, trans. J. Riviere (New York: Washington Square Press, 1960).
—— *Group Psychology and Analysis of the Ego* (London, 1922).
Galanter, E., Mandler, G., Brown, R. and Hess, E. (eds), *New Directions in Psychology* (New York: Holt, Rinehart & Winston, 1962).
Goldman, A., *A Theory of Human Action* (Englewood Cliffs: Prentice-Hall, 1970).
Gustafson, D. (ed.), *Essays in Philosophical Psychology* (Garden City: Anchor Books, 1964; London: Macmillan, 1967 .
Hampshire, S., *Freedom of the Individual* (New York: Harper & Row, 1965).
Hare, R. M., *The Language of Morals* (Oxford: Clarendon Press, 1952).

Hebb, D. O., *A Textbook of Psychology* (Philadelphia: W. B. Saunders, 1958).

Hook, S. (ed.), *Dimensions of Mind* (New York: New York University Press, 1960).

—— *Philosophy and History* (New York: New York University Press, 1963).

—— *Law and Philosophy* (New York: New York University Press, 1964).

Johnstone, H., *The Problem of the Self* (Pennsylvania State College Press, 1970).

Kaplan, A., *The Conduct of Inquiry* (San Francisco: Chandler, 1964).

Kenny, A., *Action, Emotion and Will* (London: Routledge & Kegan Paul; New York: Humanities Press, 1963).

Laing, R. D., *The Divided Self* (Baltimore: Pelican Books, 1965).

Lehrer, K. (ed.), *Freedom and Determinism* (New York: Random House, 1966).

Louch, A. R., *Explanation and Human Action* (Berkeley: University of California Press, 1966).

MacIntyre, A. C., *The Unconscious* (New York: Humanities Press, 1957).

Margolis, J., *Psychotherapy and Morality* (New York: Random House, 1966).

Melden, A. I., *Free Action* (London: Routledge & Kegan Paul; New York: Humanities Press, 1961).

Nagel, E., *The Structure of Science* (New York: Harcourt, Brace & World, 1961).

Nagel, T., *The Possibility of Altruism* (New York: Oxford University Press, 1970).

Nowell-Smith, P. H., *Ethics* (Oxford: Blackwell, 1957).

Penelhum, T., *Survival and Disembodied Existence* (New York: Humanities Press, 1970).

Peters, R., *The Concept of Motivation* (New York: Humanities Press, 1958).

Rawls, J., *A Theory of Justice* (Cambridge, Mass.: Harvard University Press, 1971).

Ruitenbeek, H. (ed.), *Psychoanalysis and Existential Philosophy* (New York: Dutton, 1962).

Ryle, G., *The Concept of Mind* (New York: Barnes and Noble, 1949).

Sartre, J.-P., *Being and Nothingness*, trans. H. Barnes (New York: Pocket Books, 1966).

—— *The Emotions, Outline of a Theory*, trans. B. Frechtman (New York: Philosophical Library, 1948).

Shoemaker, S., *Self Knowledge and Self Identity* (Ithaca: Cornell University Press, 1963).

Strawson, P. F., *Individuals* (London: Methuen, 1959).

Szasz, T. S., *The Myth of Mental Illness* (New York: Hoeber-Harper, 1961).

Taylor, C., *The Explanation of Behavior* (London: Routledge & Kegan Paul, 1964).

Taylor, R., *Action and Purpose* (Englewood Cliffs: Prentice-Hall, 1966).

Van den Berg, J. H., *The Phenomenological Approach to Psychiatry* (Springfield: Thomas, 1955).

Wann, T. W., *Behaviorism and Phenomenology* (Chicago: University of Chicago Press, 1964).

Winch, P., *The Idea of a Social Science* (New York: Humanities Press, 1958).
Wittgenstein, L., *Lectures and Conversations*, ed. C. Barrett (Berkeley: University of California Press, 1967).
—— *On Certainty*, trans. D. Paul and G. Anscombe, ed. G. Anscombe and G. von Wright (New York: Harper Torchbooks, 1969).
—— *Philosophical Investigations*, trans. G. Anscombe (New York: Macmillan, 1953).
—— *Zettel*, trans. G. Anscombe, ed. G. Anscombe and G. von Wright (Berkeley: University of California Press, 1970).

ARTICLES

Abelson, R., 'A Spade is a Spade', in *Dimensions of Mind*, ed. S. Hook (New York: New York University Press, 1960).
—— 'Because I Want to', *Mind*, 74 (1965).
—— 'Doing, Causing and Causing to do', *Journal of Philosophy*, 67 (1970).
—— 'Persons, P-Predicates and Robots', *American Philosophical Quarterly*, 3 (1966).
—— 'A Refutation of Mind-Body Identity Theory', *Philosophical Studies*, 21 (1971).
Bedford, E., 'Emotions', in *Essays in Philosophical Psychology*, ed. D. Gustafson (Garden City: Anchor Books, 1964).
Berofsky, B., 'Determinism and the Concept of a Person', *Journal of Philosophy*, 61 (1964).
Brandt, R. and Kim, J., 'Wants as Explanations of Actions', *Journal of Philosophy*, 60 (1963).
Bridges, R., 'Emotional Development in Early Infancy', in *Emotion: Bodily Change*, ed. D. K. Candland (Princeton, N.J.: Van Nostrand, 1962).
Carnap, R., 'Testability and Meaning', *Philosophy of Science*, 3 (1963).
Chisholm, R., 'Sentences about Believing', *Proceedings of the Aristotelian Society*, 56 (1955-6).
Danto, A., 'What We Can Do', *Journal of Philosophy*, 60 (1963).
—— 'Freedom and Forebearance', in *Freedom and Determinism*, ed. K. Lehrer (New York: Random House, 1966).
—— 'Basic Actions', *American Philosophical Quarterly*, 2 (1965).
—— 'Human Nature and Natural Law', in *Law and Philosophy*, ed. S. Hook (New York: New York University Press, 1964).
Davidson, D., 'Actions, Reasons and Causes', *Journal of Philosophy*, 60 (1963).
—— 'How is Weakness of the Will Possible?' in *Moral Problems*, ed. J. Feinberg (Oxford: Oxford University Press, 1969).
Duffy, E., 'An Explanation of "Emotional" Phenomena Without the Use of the Concept of Emotion', in *Emotion: Bodily Change*, ed. D. K. Candland (Princeton, N.J.: Van Nostrand, 1962).
Feigl, H., 'Mind-Body, not a Pseudoproblem', in *Dimensions of Mind*, ed. S. Hook (New York: New York University Press, 1960).
Foot, P., 'Free Will as Involving Determinism', *Philosophical Review*, 64 (1957).
Gean, W. D., 'Reasons and Causes', *Review of Metaphysics*, 19 (1966).

Gewirth, A., 'Must We Play the Moral Language Game?' *American Philosophical Quarterly*, 7 (1970).

Goldberg, B., 'Can a Desire be a Cause?' *Analysis*, 25 (1965).

Hempel, C. G., 'Reasons and Covering Laws in Historical Explanation', in *Philosophy and History*, ed. S. Hook (New York: New York University Press, 1963).

—— and Oppenheim, P., 'The Logic of Explanation', *Philosophy of Science*, 15 (1948).

Kripke, S., 'Naming and Necessity', *Semantics of Natural Language*, ed. D. Davidson and G. Harman (New York: Humanities Press, 1972).

—— 'Identity and Necessity', in *Identity and Individuation*, ed. M. K. Munitz (New York: New York University Press, 1971).

Laing, R. D., 'Ontological Insecurity', in *Psychoanalysis and Existential Philosophy*, ed. H. Ruitenbeek (New York: Dutton, 1962).

MacIntyre, A. C., 'The Antecedents of Action', in *British Analytical Philosophy*, eds B. Williams and A. Montefiore (London: Routledge & Kegan Paul; New York: Humanities Press, 1966).

Malcolm, N., 'Behaviorism as a Philosophy of Psychology', in *Behaviorism and Phenomenology*, ed. T. Wann (Chicago: University of Chicago Press, 1964).

Mullane, H., 'Psychoanalytic Explanation and Rationality', *Journal of Philosophy*, 68 (1971).

Nagel, T., 'Physicalism', *Philosophical Review*, 74 (1965).

Pears, D., 'Are Reasons for Actions Causes?' in *Epistemology*, ed. A. Stroll (New York: St Martin's Press, 1969).

—— 'Desires as Causes of Actions', in *The Human Agent: Royal Institute of Philosophy Lectures*, vol. 1 (London: Macmillan, 1968).

Prichard, H., 'Does Moral Philosophy Rest on a Mistake?' *Mind* (1912).

Putnam, H., 'Minds and Machines', in *Dimensions of Mind*, ed. S. Hook (New York: New York University Press, 1960).

—— 'Robots: Machines or Artificially Created Life?', *Journal of Philosophy*, 61 (1964).

—— 'Brains and Behavior', in *Analytical Philosophy*, ed. R. Butler, 2nd ser. (Oxford: Blackwell, 1965).

—— 'Psychological Predicates', in *Art, Mind and Religion*, ed. W. H. Capitan (Pittsburgh: Pittsburgh University Press, 1968).

Rorty, R., 'Mind-Body, Identity, Privacy and Categories', *Review of Metaphysics*, 19 (1965).

Sellars, W., 'Empiricism and the Philosophy of Mind', in *Minnesota Studies in the Philosophy of Science*, eds H. Feigl and M. Scriven, vol. 1 (Minneapolis: University of Minnesota Press, 1956).

—— 'Intentionality and the Mental', *Minnesota Studies*, vol. 11 (1958) appendix.

Smart, J. J. C., 'Sensations and Brain Processes', *Philosophical Review*, 68 (1969).

—— 'Materialism', *Journal of Philosophy*, 60–2 (1963).

# Index of Names

*The letter 'b' following a page number denotes an entry in the bibliography, and the letter 'n' an entry in a note.*

Abelson, Raziel, 129b
Alleg, Henri, 122n
Anscombe, G. E. M., xi, 2, 19, 29, 33, 119n, 120n, 127b
Aquinas, St Thomas, ix, 58
Aristotle, 58, 108
Armstrong, D. M., 127b
Aune, Bruce, 70, 120n, 127b
Austin, J. L., ix, 13, 16, 19, 29, 63, 119n, 127b
Ayer, A. J., xii, 75–81, 85, 127b

Baier, K. M., 29, 49, 111, 116, 122n, 126n, 127b
Barnes, H., 125n
Bedford, Errol, 57–8, 123n, 129b
Bennett, Philip, 122n
Berofsky, Bernard, 38, 121n, 127b, 129b
Brandt, Richard, 38, 121n, 129b
Brentano, Franz, 6
Bridges, K. M. B., 122n, 129b
Brown, R., 127b
Butler, R. J., 87, 124n, 127b, 130b

Candland, D. K., 122n, 127b
Capitan, W. H., 124n, 127b, 130b
Carnap, Rudolf, 81–2, 123n, 129b
Chisholm, Roderick, 6, 119n, 129b

Danto, A. C., xii, 98, 121n, 125n, 127b, 129b
Davidson, Donald, x, 37–41, 108, 121n, 126n, 129b
Demos, Raphael, xii
Descartes, René, 65, 79, 88, 90–1, 123n
Dewey, John, x

Downes, Chauncey, 124b
Dray, William, 29–30, 32–5, 48, 61, 120n, 127b
Dretzke, Fred, 6
Duffy, E., 58, 122n, 129b
Duns Scotus, ix

Feigl, Herbert, 69, 119n, 123n, 124n, 127b, 129b, 130b
Feinberg, Joel, 126n, 127b
Fingarette, Herbert, xii, 97, 101, 103–104, 126n, 127b
Fodor, J., 23, 120n, 127b
Foot, Philippa, 33, 120n, 129b
Frechtman, B., 123n
Freud, Sigmund, 10, 12, 45, 57, 58, 96–8, 101, 103, 104, 108, 109, 125n, 126n, 127b

Galanter, E., 122n, 127b
Gallie, W. B., 86, 125n
Gean, W. D., x, 37–8, 40–1, 121n, 129b
Gewirth, Alan, 111–15, 126n, 129b
Gibbon, Edward, 122n
Goldberg, Bruce, 37–40, 121n, 130b
Goldman, Alvin, 127b
Gustafson, Donald, xii, 123n, 127b

Hamlyn, D. W., 29
Hampshire, Stuart, 120n, 127b
Hare, R. M., 29, 86, 125n, 127b
Hebb, D. O., 1, 119n, 122n, 128b
Hegel, G. W. F., 13, 21, 117
Heidegger, Martin, 57, 58
Hempel, C., 38, 119n, 130b
Hess, E., 127b
Hitler, Adolf, 8

Hobbes, Thomas, 111, 116
Hook, Sidney, 121n, 122n, 123n, 124n, 125n, 128b, 130b
Hull, C. L., 1
Hume, David, ix, 36, 59, 74

James, William, x, 56
Jaspers, Karl, 57, 58
Johnstone, Henry W., 104, 126n, 128b

Kant, Immanuel, ix, xi, 1, 21, 59, 79, 113, 114
Kaplan, Abraham, 38, 121n, 128b
Kenny, Anthony, xi, 36, 38, 54, 56, 58, 82, 122n, 125n, 128b
Kierkegaard, Søren, 21, 57
Kim, J., 38, 121n, 129b
Koehler, Wolfgang, 70
Kripke, Saul, 71–2, 124n, 130b

Laing, R. D., 91, 104, 125n, 128b, 130b
Lehrer, Keith, 122n, 128b, 129b
Leibniz, G., ix
Locke, John, 87, 90
Louch, A. R., 128b

MacIntyre, A. C., xi, 10, 38, 45, 119n, 121n, 128b, 130b
Malcolm, Norman, 15, 16, 110, 119n, 130b
Mandler, J., 122n, 127b
Margolis, Joseph, 38, 121n, 128b
Marx, Karl, 10, 13, 21, 90, 117
Maxwell, Grover, 119n, 123n
Mayo, Bernard, 29
Meinong, A., 15
Melden, A. I., x–xii, 29–34, 36–9, 42, 48–50, 62–4, 98, 119n, 120n, 121n, 122n, 123n, 128b
Mill, J. S., 66
Miller, G., 122n
Molière, Jean-Baptiste, 11, 53
Montefiore, Alan, 121n
Moore, G. E., 16
Morick, Henry, 6
Mullane, Harvey, 61, 123n, 130b
Munitz, M. K., 124b, 130n

Nagel, Ernest, 7, 119n, 128b
Nagel, Thomas, 56–60, 111–16, 122n, 123n, 126n, 128b, 130b
Nietzsche, Friedrich, 117
Nowell-Smith, P. H., 29, 50, 122n, 128b

Oppenheim, P., 119n, 130b

Pascal, Blaise, 123n
Pears, D. F., 130b
Peirce, C. S., x
Penelhum, Terence, xii, 89, 125n, 128b
Peters, R. S., xi, 3, 29, 34, 36, 48, 61, 115, 119n, 120n, 122n, 123n, 128b
Piaget, Jean, 9
Plate, 104, 108, 111
Prichard, H. A., 111, 116, 126n, 130b
Proust, Marcel, 15
Putnam, Hilary, 70, 124n, 125n, 130b

Quine, W. V. O., 15

Rawls, John, 111, 113–14, 117, 126n, 128b
Reid, Thomas, 87
Rorty, Richard, 23–7, 120n, 123n, 130b
Rosenthal, David, 6
Rousseau, Jean-Jacques, 21
Ruitenbeek, H. M., 125n, 128b, 130b
Ryle, Gilbert, ix, xi, xii, 1, 3, 13, 15, 16, 22, 28–30, 32–4, 36, 48–52, 56–7, 59, 64, 72–3, 81, 85, 99, 100, 110–11, 119n, 120n, 122n, 125n, 126n, 128b

Sartre, Jean-Paul, xii, 4, 13, 101, 104, 107–9, 123n, 125n, 126n, 128b
Saunders, W. B., 119n
Schwartzbart, André, 122n
Scriven, Michael, 119n, 123n, 130b
Sellars, Wilfred, 6, 130b
Shoemaker, Sidney, 2, 9, 74, 87, 89, 119n, 124n, 125n, 128b
Siegler, F., xii
Skinner, B. F., 1, 2, 21, 103
Smart, J. J. C., 123n, 130b

Socrates, 110
Souverine, Boris, 122n
Spinoza, Baruch, 58
Stalin, Josef, 58, 122n
Strawson, P. F., xii, 2, 19, 26, 74–8,
　80, 84–5, 105, 119n, 124n, 125n,
　128b
Szasz, Thomas, 123n, 128b

Taylor, Charles, xi, 29, 42, 119n,
　121n, 128b
Taylor, Richard, x, xi, 33, 36–9, 41–
　47, 98, 119n, 120n, 121n, 128b
Titchener, G., 2
Toulmin, Stephen, 1, 17, 29
Trotsky, Leon, 58

Urmson, J. O., 29

Van den Berg, J. H., 123n, 128b
Veblen, Thorstein, 5

Wann, T. W., 119n, 128b
Williams, B. A. O., 121n
Winch, Peter, xi, 29, 119n, 129b
Wittgenstein, Ludwig, ix, xii, 1, 13,
　17, 19, 25–6, 28, 36–7, 48, 62, 65,
　73–4, 87, 94, 110, 117, 120n, 125n,
　129b
Wright, G. H., von 129b
Wundt, W., 2

Young, P. T., 122b

# Index of Subjects

Action, x, 1f, 13f, 88
  and event, 42, 63f
  simple or basic, 43f, 99f
  verbal, 20f
  voluntary, xf, 11, 28f, 37f, 65f, 96, 100, 116
Agency, 28f, 43f, 67, 74f
*Akrasia*, 94f, 106f
Ambiguity, 108
Analytic, 39
Anger, 4, 59, 81f
*A Priori*, 21f, 43
Authority
  cognitive, 107f
  of avowal, 9, 13f, 88f, 105f
  volitional, 107f
Avowals, x, 13f, 19f, 28, 59, 74, 85
  incorrigibility of, 15f, 24f, 118
  of 'engagements in the world', 98f

Behaviour, 75f
  abnormal, 11
  pain-, 13
Behaviourism, 2f, 21, 38
Belief, ix, 16f, 41, 74, 97f
Body, 90f
  *see also* Mind-body problem
Body-transfer, 90
Bundle theory, 74f

C-fibres, 25f, 71
Category mistake, 28
Cause, xf, 28f, 38f, 43f, 63f
  epiphenomenal, 66–7
  first, 42f
  mental, xi
  substantial, 36f, 44
  *see also* Determinism; Laws
*Ceteris paribus*, 18, 53
Character, 52f, 85

Coercion, 45–7
Community, xii, 118
Computers, 22, 70f
Concept, x, 4f
  motivational, xf, 2f, 37f
  of observables, 25f
  of person, xi, 80f
  of self, xii, 87f, 104f, 115f
  physical, 22
  psychological, 1f, 22f, 37f, 80f
  'status', xii
Conflict, 108–9
Consciousness, 10, 74f, 104
  *see also* Unconscious
Criteria, 37, 61, 75f, 81f
  behavioural, 75, 81f, 105
  of persons, 79f, 87f

Democracy, 21
Desire, xi, 29f, 50f, 55f, 65f
  unconscious, 55
Determinism, ixf, 7, 30, 37f, 117
  incoherence of, 62f
  'soft', 65f
Dialectic, 97f, 102, 104f
Discrete state theory, 70f
Disposition, 48, 50f, 59f, 81f
Doing
  and causing, 36f, 41f
  *see also* Action, voluntary
Dreams, 14f
Dual aspect theory, xi
Dualism, ix, 29, 65f, 88f
  'conceptual', ixf, 1f, 29f
  *see also* Interactionism; Mind-body problem
Duty, 112f

Ego, superego and id, 96, 101
Ego ideal, 103

Egoism, 114f
Emotion, ix, xi, 4, 29f, 57f, 83f
  moral 59, 82
  simulated 83
Encephalography, 25f
Enjoyment, 48, 51f
Entailment, 23, 40, 81
  'contextual', x, 40, 53, 81f
Ethics, ix, x, 34
  *see also* Morality
Evaluation, xi, 3f, 11, 13f, 23f, 85f
Event, *see* Action, and event
Evidence, 19, 89
  avoidance of, 95f, 101
Explanation
  *ad hoc*, 96
  causal, xf, 10f, 28f, 38f, 62f
  deductive model of, 4
  pseudo-, 8
  psychological, xf, 7f, 11, 30, 53f
  purposive, 7f, 11, 30, 53
  rational, 38f, 52f
  scientific, ix
  vacuous, 11

Faith, ix
Fear, 4f, 46
Feeling, ix, xi, 55f, 84f
Freedom, xif, 27, 117
  of will, 62f
  to avow, 13f, 2of
'Functional states', 7of

Generalisation, 14f, 22f
Goals, 54f, 60, 115
'Grammatical accusatives', 16

Hypnosis, 45–6
Hypothetical constructs, 23

Identity theory, xi, 62, 67f
Images, *see* Memory
Incontinence, 108f
Incorrigibility, *see* Avowals, incor-
  rigibility of
Indeterminism, xi, 37f, 62f
Insincerity, 27, 95f
Intention, 37f, 47, 56, 65
Intentionality, x, 2, 6f, 14, 56, 105

Interactionism, 64f
Introspection, 2f, 76, 80

Jealousy, 58–9
Judgment
  categorical, 108f
  moral, 112f
  normative, ixf, 2f, 14, 29f, 48
  *prima facie* and *sans phrase*, 108f
  prudential, 112f
Justification, 32f, 48, 114f

Knowledge, ix, x
  non-observational, 2f, 19f, 28, 88f
  of motives, 31f
  psychological, 13f
  *see also* Self-knowledge

Language
  evaluative, 86f
  game, x
  of action, xf, 1f, 36f
  of science, 1f, 10f, 36f
  psychological, 78f
  uses of, 17f
Laws, xf, 4f, 48, 62f
  behavioural, 4, 30, 81
  causal, xi, 8
Libertarianism, 73
Logical connection argument, x, 37f
Love, 18–19, 48
  concept of, 23–4

*Mauvaise foi*, 103, 107
Means-ends, 53f
  rules governing, 55
Mechanism, ix, 30, 50
Memory, 14f, 99f
Metaphor, 97f, 106f
Mind-body problem, ixf, 67f, 75, 90f
Morality, xii, 111f, 118
Motive, xf, 29f, 37f, 48f, 65f
  unconscious, 10f
Multiple-agent model, 96f

Necessary and sufficient conditions,
  xii, 20, 68–9, 75f, 82f
Need, 51
Neurology, 25f
Noumenon, xi

Number theory, 68

'Ontological insecurity', 91f
Open texture, 81, 87
Ordinary language, 41
Other minds problem, 79f

P-predicates, 75f
Pain, 13, 18, 25f, 48, 84
    behaviour, 25f
Paradox
    epistemic, 95f, 99f
    of *akrasia*, 108–9
    of mind-body, 111
    of reflexivity, 104f
    psycho-ethical, 97f, 107
Perception, 3, 16f
Performatives, 19f, 28
Person status, 76f, 86f
Personal identity, 74f, 87f
Phenomenological reports, 14f
Physics, 1f, 10f
Physiology, 1f, 57
Pleasure and pain, 4
Prediction, 11, 37, 52
Privileged access, 2f, 19f
'Probabilistic automata', 70
Psychiatry, 34–5, 57
Psychoanalysis, 10, 45, 58, 96
Psychology, xf, 1f, 10f, 49f, 58
Psychotherapy, 11, 91f, 110

Reasons, ixf, 4f, 11, 28f, 37f, 58f, 74f,
    83, 112f
    good, 32f, 49
    *prima facie*, xii
    self-regarding, 49f
    subjective and objective, 112f
    unconscious, 61
Reason-terminating locutions, xi, 51f,
    115
Reductionism, 65f, 76f, 80
'Reduction sentences', 81f
Reference, 13
    rigid, 71–2
Reinforcement, 3
REM experiments, 16
Responsibility, xif, 118
Rigid designators, 71f

Rights, xii, 20–1, 26, 114f
    and interests, xii, 114f
Robots, 23, 77f, 85
Rules
    of action, 54f, 103
    semantical and syntactical, 18,
        84

Science, ix, 1f, 58
    natural, ix, 13f
    social, x
    *see also* Language, of science;
        Physics; Psychology
Self, xii, 74f, 87f, 101f, 104f, 110f
    -amputation, xii, 97f, 102
    as project, 93f
    -deception, 9, 93, 94f, 114
    description, 14f
    ideal, 103f, 107f, 116f
    -interest, xii, 108f, 111f
    -knowledge xii, 2f, 10f, 14f, 74f
        99f, 110f
    multiple-, xii, 97f
    -reference, xii, 87f
    -scrutiny, 99
    two concepts of, 87f, 102f, 107f,
        115f
Solipsism, 113, 117
Soul, 87f
Standards, 4f
Stimulus-response, 3f
Substance theory, 74f

Theory
    of motivation, 9f
    psychoanalytic, 9f, 45
Trying, 89

Unconscious, 10, 23, 45f, 55, 57, 61,
    97
Use
    avowal-, 17f
    expressive, 17f
    grammatical reflexive, 87
    normative, 86–7
    performative, 19f
    phenomenological, 17f
    philosophical, 93
    reflexive, 87f

Values, xi, 21, 56, 116
  and facts, 5
  relative, 117
  universal, 103, 116
*Vera causa*, 66–7
Verification, 6, 10, 14, 61

Volition, 36f, 43f, 65f, 97

Wanting, ix, 9, 18, 40, 48f, 55f, 108f
Weakness of will, *see Akrasia*
Will, *see* Action, voluntary; Freedom
  of will; Volition